The Complete Book of
Papercrafts

The Complete Book of
Papercrafts

26 step-by-step projects made from paper

David & Charles

A DAVID & CHARLES BOOK

First published in the UK in 2002
Copyright © David & Charles 2002

Distributed in North America
by F&W Publications, Inc.
4700 E. Galbraith Rd.
Cincinnati, OH 45236
1-800-289-0963

A catalogue record for this book is available from the British Library.

ISBN 0 7153 1231 6

Commissioning editor   Fiona Eaton
Art editor   Lisa Forrester
Project editor   Jennifer Proverbs
Production controller   Jennifer Campbell

Printed in Thailand by Imago
for David & Charles
Brunel House   Newton Abbot   Devon

The techniques and projects in this book previously appeared as part of the
Crafts Made Easy series, published by David & Charles

Contents

INTRODUCTION

Paper is one of the most accessible, versatile and fun media for today's crafter. It is easy to work with and requires no specialist equipment or knowledge, yet professional-looking results are simple to obtain. A huge choice is available – from rough, organic textures to metallic, patterned or corrugated card in a riot of colours. Unlike so many other craft materials, making your own paper is both simple and rewarding (see pages 10–19).

The six techniques at the beginning of the book, encompassing decorative papers, 3-D découpage, greetings cards, papier mâché, stamping and stencilling, provide everything you need to know in order to tackle any of the projects. The projects themselves offer a diverse and exciting choice, for the beginner and more experienced crafter alike, including greetings cards, gift presentation ideas, stationery and decorative items.

Greetings cards (page 60) are one of the most obvious items to make from paper, something that we first do as children for birthdays, anniversaries and a whole range of other occasions. The Miniature Scrap Ideas on page 66 provide ways to experiment with a range of papers, combining colours and textures with other materials. Stamping and découpage used together produce an eye-catching, three-dimensional greetings card on page 70.

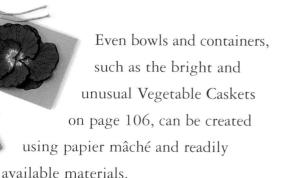

If you have made a special greetings card for a friend or relative, why not give them their present wrapped in giftpaper or in a gift bag or box you have made yourself?

Even bowls and containers, such as the bright and unusual Vegetable Caskets on page 106, can be created using papier mâché and readily available materials.

Gift Presentation (page 92) includes ideas for gift-wrap and tags, such as the gorgeous Lacy Wrapping on page 94. The strikingly shaped and decorated gift tags are easy and quick to make, and several techniques can be used to obtain the finish you want.

Paper is a natural material to use for making stationery and desk accessories, and a whole range of projects offers stunning ideas (page 124). The pen tidies, photo album and even a pretty paper-covered stationery box (page 148) will add colour and interest to any desk.

Beautifully handmade and embellished items look wonderful in any home, and make unusual gifts that will be treasured. There are plenty of ideas in this book for making articles that are attractive and often practical. They include a marbled picture frame, a Native American-inspired,

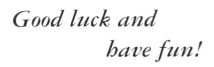

papier mâché tray (page 160) and a set of patterned storage boxes you won't want to hide. Once again, there is a varied range of techniques used throughout, and all the materials are so accessible and simple to customize.

Choose a project you would like to make, then learn the technique used to complete it by following the clear step-by-step instructions. Be confident and explore papercrafts – with so many projects and techniques to choose from, you will be an expert in no time!

Good luck and have fun!

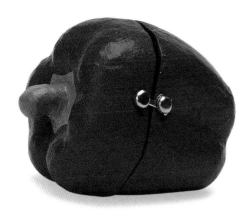

Decorative Papers
TOOLS, MATERIALS AND TECHNIQUES

Essential equipment

Below is a list of equipment needed for paper making and decorating:

- **Mould and deckle**: two identical wooden frames, one covered with net, that fit exactly together and are used to collect paper pulp from the vat
- **Vat**: a plastic tray, larger than the mould and deckle, that will hold sufficient paper pulp to make a sheet of paper
- **Bucket**: used for soaking scrap paper to make paper pulp
- **Length of wood or hand liquidizer**: used for beating the paper pulp to a smooth, creamy paste
- **Hardboard**: used to sandwich the newly made stack of paper
- **Clean bricks or heavy weights**: used on top of the hardboard to apply pressure to the stack of paper
- **Kitchen cloths**: used between each sheet of paper to soak up the water, and make it easier to move while wet
- **Plastic sheet**: to cover your work surface
- **Newspaper**: to protect your work surface
- **Rolling pin**: to give the wet sheets of paper a smooth finish
- **Paintbrush**: for applying paint over batik wax and to decorate paste paper
- **Saucepan or double boiler**: for making vegetable paper, and heating batik wax
- **Empty food can**: for melting and pouring batik wax

Making coloured paper

Paper pulp can be made from coloured waste paper or from plain pulp coloured with a small amount of strong-coloured paper, natural colouring or dye.

- **Recycling coloured paper**
  Use crackers, napkins, tissue, crêpe, wrapping paper and paper bags

- **Colouring the pulp**
  Juice from soft fruit like blackberries, raspberries, strawberries and blackcurrants
  Vegetable juice, particularly from carrots and beetroots, boiled onion skins
  Spices like curry powder, turmeric, chilli powder and cinnamon
  Leaf and fruit tea
  Instant coffee
  Powdered poster paint and drawing ink
  Food colouring, both powdered and liquid
- **Colouring the finished paper**
  Food colouring
  Fruit and vegetable juice
  Poster paint, silk paint, acrylic paint and ink

Tips for making paper

- ✔ Use a plastic sheet and plenty of newspaper to protect your work surface
- ✔ Clean the mould and deckle thoroughly between making each sheet of paper
- ✔ Use a cat litter tray as a vat for making paper and for marbling
- ✔ Let as much water drain away as possible before you transfer the newly made sheet of paper to the kitchen cloth
- ✔ Adjust the ratio of pulp to water in the vat between making each sheet, so that you have one third pulp to two thirds water

Textured paper

Use some of these techniques to create paper with a textured surface:

- ✔ Leave the paper to dry on textured fabric like tweed, a lace mat or patterned net curtain
- ✔ Push objects into the damp paper to make a raised pattern
- ✔ Add dried lentils and split peas to the pulp
- ✔ Add scraps of material, wool, raffia and ribbon to the pulp
- ✔ Add ribbon roses, beads, metal foil and scraps of paper to the surface of the pulp
- ✔ Drop pressed flowers and leaves, seeds and potpourri on to the pulp

Surface decoration

- **Marbling:** use marbling ink or oil paint to create a swirly pattern on the paper
- **Batik:** use melted wax and paint to create a resist pattern
- **Paste:** scratch a pattern on the paper in a layer of wallpaper paste and paint
- **Fold 'n' dye:** Fold Japanese paper, then dip it in dye or paint

Making pulp

How to choose the right paper

- Recycle paper with long fibres (see below), as this will make the strongest paper
- Tear the paper to see if there are wispy fibres on the tear: these are the long fibres
- Avoid heavily printed paper, glossy magazines or mailshots
- Newspaper should be avoided because the printing ink creates a black scum on the surface of the pulp
- Avoid paper with a shiny surface as it may be coated with clay, and will leave powdery patches on the finished paper
- Do not use paper that has been glued
- Remove tape and staples before using the paper

Types of paper to recycle

- Computer print-out paper ● old envelopes ● paper bags ● wrapping paper ● paper napkins ● tissue paper ● Christmas decorations (crackers, paper hats, streamers) ● crêpe paper ● photocopier paper

Making paper from plants

- Use stringy, narrow-leaved plants like leeks, rhubarb, celery, cow parsley, fennel, rushes, reeds, grasses, irises and daffodil leaves

- Use pineapple tops, cabbage peelings, cauliflower leaves, onion skins and nettles

Making a Mould and Deckle

To make paper you will need to buy or make a mould and deckle. These two identical wooden frames, one covered with net, act like a sieve, collecting paper pulp whilst draining away the water. Use old net curtain or fine dressmaking net to cover the mould, stretching it tightly before stapling it at the edges

1 Cut four pieces of 2x1cm (^{3}/$_4$x^3/$_8$in) thick timber 27cm (10^3/$_4$in) long, and four pieces 20cm (8in) long. Arrange two longer, and two shorter pieces together to make the mould. Use PVA glue to hold the pieces together. Use the other four pieces to make the deckle.

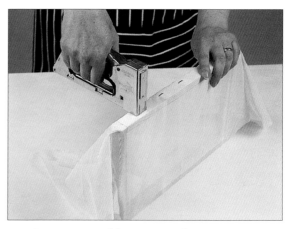

3 Cut a piece of fine net to fit over the mould. Wet the net and attach it to the frame using steel staples. Start by stapling the middle of each side, pulling as tightly as you can. Staple around the frame pulling the net taut. As the net dries it will become tighter.

2 Once the glue is dry, hammer two rust-proof nails into each corner of the mould, making sure they are long enough to go into both lengths of wood. Repeat for the deckle.

4 Cut away the excess net, and then seal the edges with waterproof PVA glue. The deckle and mould should be exactly the same size when held together.

Making a Sheet of Paper

Almost any paper can be recycled, but pulp containing long fibres makes the best paper. Computer print-out paper, paper bags and envelopes are excellent – because they need to be strong they are made from long fibres. To check the length of the fibres, tear the paper and if it has long wispy ends it will make good paper

1 Prepare the paper to be recycled by removing all traces of glue and taking out any staples. Avoid paper with a shiny surface as this can cause powdery patches on the finished paper. Tear the paper into small squares about the size of a postage stamp.

3 The wet paper needs to be beaten to a mushy pulp using a piece of wood or a hand-held liquidizer. If there is too much water remaining in the bucket, tip some away before beating. The pulp needs to be very smooth and creamy.

2 Put the torn paper into a bucket of water and leave to soak for a few days. You may need to top up the water as it gets drawn into the paper.

4 Half fill a plastic tray (the vat) with water, add the pulp and stir well until mixed. Adjust the ratio of pulp to water until you have one third pulp to two thirds water.

5 Paper making uses a lot of water, so it is important to protect your working surface, floor and clothing. Spread several layers of newspaper in the area where you will be working. Now place a pad of folded newspaper in the centre. On top of this, place a thin piece of hardboard, and then cover with a damp kitchen cloth. Smooth the cloth flat to stop marks being transferred to the finished paper.

7 Push the mould and deckle slowly, and at an angle, into the pulp, working from the far side of the vat. As you push further into the pulp, so more will be collected on to the net. If you have trouble collecting the pulp on the net, the ratio of pulp to water may be wrong and will need adjusting. Too much pulp and the paper will be thick and lumpy, too little and it will be thin and holey.

6 Give the pulp another good stir. Place the deckle on top of the mould, with the net side uppermost and lining up the edges exactly. Grip the shorter edges, pressing the pieces firmly together. The deckle will stop the pulp running off the mould and give the paper neat straight edges.

8 Straighten up the mould and deckle so that the net is just below the surface of the pulp. Gently lift the mould and deckle to check that you have an even thickness of pulp on the net. If you are unhappy with the spread of pulp, scrape it back into the vat and start again.

9 Lift the mould and deckle right out of the pulp, and then gently rock it backwards and forwards and from side to side. This will help to settle the fibres and give a flat, even sheet of paper. Do not overdo the rocking or the pulp will become holey. Allow the excess water to drain away; this can take several minutes, so balance the mould and deckle across one corner of the vat.

10 Take away the deckle from the top of the mould. Some water may have been caught around the inside edges of the deckle; allow this to drain, keeping the mould flat until the water has gone. Turn the mould over so that the newly made sheet of paper faces downwards.

11 Although the paper will be held reasonably firmly on the net, it is advisable to transfer the paper to the kitchen cloth quickly. If the paper falls off the mould, scrape it back into the vat and make the sheet again. In one gentle rolling movement, place the mould on to the cloth, press down on one short edge, and lift up on the opposite edge.

12 Roll the mould up and away, leaving the sheet of paper on the kitchen cloth. You may need a few goes to get an even layer of paper on the net, and to get the paper to stay on the kitchen cloth when you roll the mould away. If things go wrong, put the pulp back into the vat and start again.

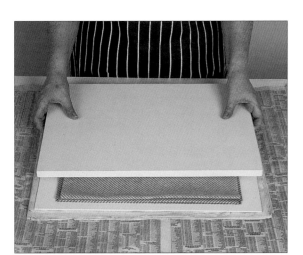

13 Place a damp kitchen cloth on top of the sheet of paper. Smooth the cloth, removing any wrinkles and making sure the surface is perfectly flat. Make four or five more sheets, and place them on top of the first with a damp kitchen cloth between each. Cover the final sheet with a damp cloth, and then cover the stack with a clean piece of hardboard.

15 Place a sheet of plastic on your work surface. Remove the board and the cloth from the top of the stack. Carefully take off a kitchen cloth with its sheet of paper, and lay it on the plastic sheet to dry. The paper will be very strong at this stage, so do not worry too much about damage. Depending on the thickness of pulp, the paper may take three or four days to dry.

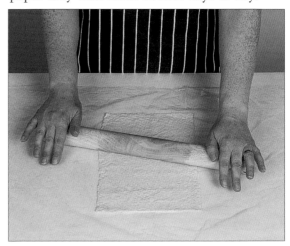

14 Place two clean bricks on top of the stack and leave for several hours until quite a lot of the excess water has been soaked up into the cloth or has run out on to the paper. This process is called 'couching', and is the point in paper making where you stack, press and dry the newly made paper.

16 If you want the paper to have a smooth surface, you will need to roll it flat while slightly damp. Use a rolling pin to give it a flat smooth surface, but do not press too hard or the paper may tear. Once pressed, dry the sheets separately under weights, such as heavy books, layering the paper between dry cloths.

Making Decorative Paper

Once you have mastered the art of making plain paper, try adding decoration using things found in your kitchen cupboards or around the house: fruit juice, thread and material scraps, coloured napkins, food colouring and fruit and vegetable peelings, all make wonderfully textured and coloured paper at very little cost

Making floral paper

Drop dried petals and leaves on to the surface of the pulp before making each sheet of paper or, to give the paper more colour, stir crushed potpourri into the pulp.

Making Christmas paper

Cut paper napkins or coloured paper into small pieces and stir them into the pulp: the dye will come out and colour the pulp. Add tinsel and glitter for a sparkly Christmas effect.

Making scrap thread paper

Cut material, ribbon and thread into small pieces and sprinkle them on the surface of the pulp. Try adding ribbon roses, metal foil and dried pulses for a more three-dimensional look.

Making coloured paper

Add food colouring, spices, instant coffee, onion skins boiled in water, and fruit tea to the pulp to make pale-coloured paper. For a brighter colour use poster paint.

Making juice-coloured paper

Fruit juice can be used to colour pulp and will give a reasonably strong result. Bring soft fruit like blackberries, blackcurrants and raspberries to the boil in a small amount of water. Simmer for a few minutes and then remove from the heat; allow to cool. Strain off the juice and stir into the pulp.

Making vegetable paper

Dissolve washing soda in a pan of water; add chopped-up plant material. Bring the water to the boil and then simmer for three quarters of an hour. Drain the pulp through a net, and then rinse under the cold tap. Beat to a smooth pulp, then make a sheet of paper following the instructions on pages 14 and 15.

Making paste paper

Paint a generous layer of wallpaper paste over the surface of a sheet of paper. Apply several colours of acrylic paint to the paste, then blend the colours together using a soft paintbrush. Use its blunt end to draw patterns in the wet paste. Dry over the slats of an airing cupboard.

Making fold 'n' dye paper

Concertina-fold a sheet of Japanese paper. Dip the sides of the folded paper into food colouring, ink or silk paint: the dye will create patterns on the paper. Cover the damp paper with a sheet of clean paper and press to remove the excess dye. Dry flat, then cover with clean paper and iron on a low heat.

Making batik paper

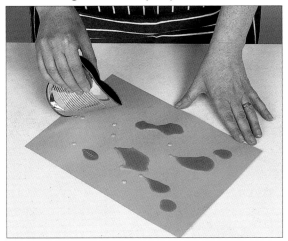

1 Melt batik wax in the top of a double boiler. Put the liquid wax in an empty food tin, squashing the sides together to form a spout. Make patterns by pouring the wax on to a sheet of pale-coloured paper or white paper painted with watery poster paint. As the wax makes contact with the paper, it will dry almost immediately.

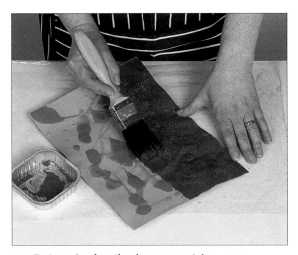

2 Paint the batiked paper with watery paint using long brush strokes: the paint will not stick to the wax. Once the paper is dry, sandwich it between newspaper. Turn the iron to a cotton setting and iron the paper – the melted wax will be absorbed into the newspaper, leaving a pattern.

Making marbled paper

1 Three quarters fill a vat with wallpaper paste and leave it to stand until the paste reaches room temperature (about ½ hour). Using a teaspoon, drop small amounts of different coloured paint on to the surface of the paste – you can use marbling paints or oils mixed with turpentine. Swirl the paint around, taking care that it stays on top of the paste.

2 Lower a sheet of paper gently on to the surface of the paste – this will prevent air bubbles forming on the surface. Then take the paper out of the vat and lay it on newspaper. Hold the marbled surface under cold running water, preferably a shower spray. Dry on a washing line, then flatten under weights.

3-D Découpage
TOOLS, MATERIALS AND TECHNIQUES

Essential equipment

Below is a list of equipment needed for
3-D découpage:

- **Scissors**: used for cutting out the design
- **Craft knife and cutting mat**: used for cutting intricate detail
- **Tweezers**: used for positioning the paper pieces onto silicone blobs
- **Cocktail stick**: used for nudging the paper pieces into position
- **Small coin**: used to check the distance between the layers is the same
- **Barbecue skewer**: used for making a bridge on the back of narrow paper pieces
- **Thin florist's wire**: used to strengthen very narrow pieces of paper
- **Spray adhesive**: for attaching the base layer of the picture
- **Newspaper**: used for covering your work surface when using spray adhesive
- **PVA or white craft glue**: used for gluing parts of the design together
- **Silicone rubber adhesive or sticky pads**: used for attaching and spacing the layers
- **Felt-tipped pens**: for colouring the cut edges of coloured paper pieces
- **Soft pencil**: for colouring the cut edges of light paper pieces
- **Shaping tool and mat or spoon**: for shaping the top layer of the picture
- **Ruler**: used as a guide when cutting straight lines
- **Paintbrush**: for applying watercolours

What to use

Below is a list of items that may be a good source for 3-D découpage:

- **Gift-wrap**: use good quality paper with multiple images and well defined edges
- **Wallpaper**: images must stand out well from the background and be close together

- **Fabric**: use lightweight furnishing fabric with a tight weave, close pattern repeat and strong single images
- **Colour photocopies**: use the stiffest paper that will work in the photocopier
- **Stamps**: choose stamps with good clear images and plenty of space for colouring
- **Photographs**: choose your subject with care: landscapes with well defined edges work best. Use matt prints and colour the edges
- **Watercolour paper**: use the thinnest paper available, which can be painted, cut out and then assembled
- **Coloured or crinkle paper and card**: 3-D découpage does not have to be restricted to pre-printed images. Use plain paper or card to make simple pictures

Useful hints and tips

✔ Attach the base layer using spray adhesive
✔ Always apply silicone using a cocktail stick
✔ Position the paper pieces using tweezers
✔ Never press down on the paper pieces being attached or the silicone will spread
✔ Use a small coin to check that the layers are the same distance apart
✔ Cut the paper using small sharp scissors and the intricate detail using a craft knife
✔ Colour the cut edges of the paper pieces
✔ Varnish will protect the paper from dust
✔ Overcut a piece if it will be partially hidden behind a subsequent layer (see page 23)

Special effects

✔ Use feathering on the edge of birds' feathers and cut animal fur using the furring technique (see page 23)
✔ Add highlights to the top layer of a picture using varnish
✔ If you have a paper piece that is narrow and difficult to position, make a wooden bridge from a barbecue skewer to support it

✔ If the piece is very narrow, like a flower stem, make a bridge from fine wire
✔ Build another scene behind a window or door for a greater feeling of distance
✔ Add shape to the top layer of a picture by making the paper concave or convex using a special tool or spoon

How to display your work

Here are some useful tips for helping you choose the right way to display your 3-D découpage.

● **Pictures**
    Use a recessed frame
    A mount can be used in front of the picture or in between the layers
    Attach the base layer to a backing board using spray adhesive
    Use handmade paper behind the design for an interesting effect
    Attach the layers on silicone blobs or sticky pads
    Glass will keep the picture dust free

● **Greetings cards**
    Use ready-made card blanks or make your own from thin card
    Silicone blobs will give a stronger finish
    If you want to put the card into an envelope, use just a few layers, or build the layers on tabs that can be flattened

● **Baubles**
    Choose clear plastic ones with a flat circular surface for applying the base layer
    Come in several different sizes
    Use silicone blobs or sticky pads

● **Gift tags**
    Use ready-made tags or make your own – parcel labels are cheap and very strong
    Silicone blobs will give a stronger finish

● **Lampshades**
    Must be made of paper or fabric-covered paper
    Must have a flat surface
    Attach the layers using silicone

● **Gift holders**
    Use ready-made paper gift bags or boxes
    Make your own cards from gift-wrap or wallpaper, and boxes from stiff card

● **Boxes**
    Use cardboard or wooden boxes
    Can be painted to match the design
    The layers can be displayed on the top or sides

Planning and Cutting

Perspective is the most important part of creating a three-dimensional picture. Remember to plan and construct the picture from the base layer: this means the items in the foreground will be the last to be positioned. When a subject extends behind a subsequent layer, it should be cut larger to avoid the edges being seen

Planning your 3-D

Look at the picture and decide what is at the back, middle and front. Cut a complete picture: this is the base layer. Then cut out the other layers, working from the back.

Cutting with scissors

Cut around shapes with small sharp scissors. Use the middle of the blades, and turn the scissors, not the paper. Avoid cutting curves as a series of straight lines.

Cutting with a knife

1 Use a craft knife and cutting mat to cut intricate detail. The knife should have a straight, sharp-pointed blade, and you should change the blade if it starts to pull on the paper. Make definite cuts in the paper, following the outlines.

2 If the cut does not go right through the paper, cut the line again. Do not pull the pieces apart or you will be left with a ragged edge and the picture will be ruined.

Overcutting

When cutting layers that will be partially hidden behind subsequent layers, cut the design larger and include a small amount of overlapping subject. When the upper layer is positioned on top, the cut edge of the lower subject will be well hidden below the upper layer.

Receding background

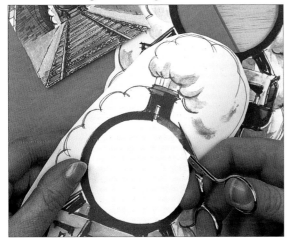

On some subjects you can achieve a greater feeling of distance by building another scene behind the main picture. This can be done where there is a window or doorway; or like the train above, where the scene continues behind the main picture. Always make sure you overcut the parts to be receded.

Feathering

Holding the scissors in one hand, turn your wrists inward, tilting the heels of both thumbs downwards and towards each other. This will lay the scissors at an acute angle, almost touching the paper. As you cut, the paper will curl: the finer the cuts, the more realistic the feathers will look.

Furring

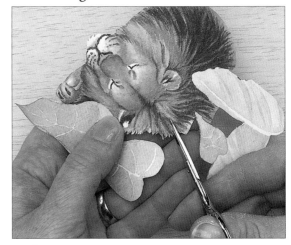

In furring, the paper should have a square edge, not round, and very little curl. First, cut away the areas of paper that are not part of the design then, holding the scissors at right angles to the paper, make short, straight cuts of varying lengths. This will give realistic-looking animal fur.

Building a Picture

When building a three-dimensional picture line up the layers exactly, with no more than a shadow of the underneath piece showing. Use blobs of silicone or self-adhesive sticky pads to space the layers apart, taking care not to get them too close, or to give them too much height, so losing the perspective and realism of the picture

Building layers

1 Silicone rubber adhesive is very similar to the sealant used around baths and wash basins. It dries almost clear and does not run or shrink. Use the end of a cocktail stick to apply 5mm (¼in) blobs to the base layer, not to the paper piece you are adding.

3 Use a cocktail stick to nudge each paper piece gently into position; try to get the piece exactly over the shape underneath. The silicone will take about half an hour to dry completely, so you will have ample time to adjust the position.

2 Position each paper piece on to a silicone blob using tweezers; do not press the paper down, or you will flatten the picture and the silicone will spread.

4 Try to get the right height between layers – too little will not look three-dimensional and too much will make the pieces float. A gap the thickness of a coin is a good guide.

Self-adhesive pads

For pictures cut from card, or to make it easier for children to enjoy 3-D découpage, self-adhesive sticky pads can be used to build up the layers. Cut the pads into small pieces, then peel off the backing paper on one side, and press the pad in position. Remove the top protective paper before adding the next layer.

Paper tabs

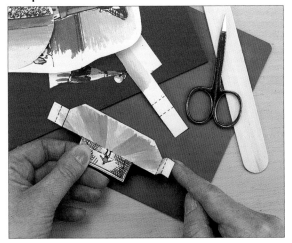

Tabs are only suitable for a picture where they will be hidden behind another layer. Extend the paper pieces at the edges by drawing and cutting tabs; when scored, folded and positioned, the tabs will give the pieces enough height to form a bridge over the previous layer.

Wooden bridge

If you have a paper piece that is narrow and difficult to position, it will help to support the area before attaching it. Glue a wooden bridge, cut from a cocktail stick or barbecue skewer, on to the back, then you will need fewer blobs of silicone, which can be positioned where they will not show.

Wire supports

Use this technique when you have a very thin piece of paper to support, like a flower stem. Bend a length of thin wire into the shape of the stem, looping it at the top and bottom for added strength. Apply white tacky glue to the back of the paper and press the wire firmly in position.

Finishing Techniques

These extra, special finishing touches will give your projects a more professional look: shaping the top layer of the design, particularly on floral subjects, will give it depth and interest; cut edges can be coloured to stop them showing; and a coat of varnish will seal the finished picture and keep it free from dust

Shaping and curving

Shape the top layer by laying it on a mat, and rubbing it with a shaping tool or spoon. Which side of the paper you work on will depend how you want the paper to curve.

Varnishing

Your finished picture can be varnished using a paper varnish; small areas can be coated with clear nail varnish. Apply the varnish thinly, in small areas, building up the coats.

Colouring edges

All the edges of the pieces should be shaded to hide the white cut paper. Use toning felt-tipped pens on coloured paper, and a soft pencil if the subject has a sketched outline.

Mounting

A recessed frame is needed to display your finished picture. This can be made to size or bought ready-made from craft suppliers. Glass will protect the picture from dust.

Sourcing Different Images

As well as pictures specially printed for 3-D use, you can source printed images from elsewhere: wallpaper and gift-wrap can be used if printed with a repeat pattern. Use good quality paper; thin paper may curl up when cut. Multiple images may also be produced using a rubber stamp; these can then be coloured

Using Stamps

Choose stamps with clear images and plenty of space for adding colour. Stamp multiple images, then colour using felt-tipped pens, before cutting out the layers (see also page 44).

Using wallpaper

Use wallpaper or borders where the images that you will be using stand out well against the background and are close together, or you will need lots of the paper.

Using fabric

Use lightweight furnishing fabric with a tight weave, close pattern repeat and strong single images. Iron interfacing on to the back before cutting the fabric.

Using gift-wrap

Wrapping paper is readily available, and if chosen carefully can make a good subject for 3-D work. Use good quality paper with multiple images and well defined edges.

Greetings Cards

TOOLS, MATERIALS AND TECHNIQUES

Essential equipment

Below is a list of equipment needed for making cards:

- **Card or thick paper**: strong enough to stand up when decorated, but thin enough to score and fold
- **Ruler**: to measure and to provide a straight edge for cutting
- **Craft knife and cutting mat**: to cut a card mount neatly and accurately
- **Sharp scissors**: to cut fabric, paper and metal sheeting
- **Pencil**: for drawing the shape of the card before cutting
- **White paper**: for making a folded insert to put inside a card
- **Double-sided tape**: for applying surface decoration or for gluing an insert in a card

- **Tacky glue**: for applying decoration to a card, envelope or tag
- **Glue gun**: for attaching heavier objects like jewels, tiles and beads to the front of a card, envelope or tag

Materials for making cards

Almost any material can be used to make a card, but the important things to remember when making your selection are: the way the card will be folded; whether there will be a window opening; and the weight and size of the surface decoration. All these things will effect the balance and stability of the card, and should be considered when choosing the material to be used.

- **Thin card**
  This is the most useful material for making cards. It comes in a wide range of colours and weights, and can be used for single- or double-folded cards with three panels, both with or without a window opening
- **Thick paper**
  This can be used in the same way as the thin card, but it may need to be folded in half and then half again to make a double-layered, single-folded card
- **Thick watercolour paper**
  Strong but very thick, so use as a single-folded card, with or without a window opening
- **Thick handmade paper**
  Use it to make a single-folded card, with torn edges
- **Corrugated card**
  This is not the same product that is used to wrap parcels, but a stronger, coloured version of the card available from craft shops. Use it for a single-folded card, without a window

Tips for making cards

✔ Measure and cut the rectangle of paper to be used for the card very accurately, making sure the corners are exact 90° angles

✔ Use the back (blunt side) of a craft knife to score the fold lines

✔ Make sure you enlarge or reduce all the tracings for each project in this book by the same percentage

✔ Use a ballpoint pen to draw design lines on to foam sheet, and always cut using a craft knife and cutting mat

✔ Use scissors to cut metal sheeting

✔ Punch holes in metal sheeting using a punching tool, on a soft wooden board with a rubber mallet

✔ Patterns can be embossed on to the back of metal sheeting using a blunt pencil or an empty ballpoint pen

✔ When using a ruler to draw lines with a metallic pen, turn it on to its convex side as this will stop the ink from spreading

✔ Wet the edges of handmade paper before tearing

✔ Odd earrings or a backless brooch can be used to decorate cards

✔ Use Blu-tack to temporarily attach a bead, stone or other heavy object to the front of a card to check the balance, and if necessary adjust the weight of the paper used for the card

✔ Always use flexible glass paint in a tube when working on acetate, then when the paint is dry and the acetate bends, the paint will not peel off the acetate

✔ Use deckle-edged scissors to give card edges a decorative finish

✔ Hang a mobile behind a window opening using invisible embroidery thread

✔ Use a glue gun to attach heavy decorative objects to cards and tags

Adding decoration

Here are just a few of the items that can be used to decorate cards:

● Foam, cork
● Metal sheeting, metal cut from food tins
● Fabric, ribbon, lace, hessian
● Jewels, mirrors and old jewellery
● Shells, stones, beads, buttons, mosaic tiles
● Dried flowers, bark, twigs, leaves, raffia
● Pompoms, chenille sticks, toy eyes
● Psychedelic paper, handmade paper
● Cake decorations, silk or paper flowers
● Outliner paste, glass paint, glitter glue
● Watercolour pencils, metallic pens
● Corrugated card, metallic card

Card accessories

● **Tags**: use the same material as the card, and a small part of the card design

● **Envelopes**: use thick paper in a colour which tones with the card, adding decoration to the front and back flap
● **Presentation box**: if the card is heavy, or has a lot of decoration, send it in a presentation box. Cover a recycled box with toning paper and decorate to match the card
● **Gift bag**: make a gift or party bag using matching paper, and then add decoration to match the card

Making a Card Mount

You need no special equipment to make professional-looking card mounts at home, just a pencil, sharp craft knife, a straight-edge and a cutting mat or board. The card you choose needs to be thick enough to stand up when decorated, but thin enough to fold on the score. Accurate cutting and folding will ensure a good finish

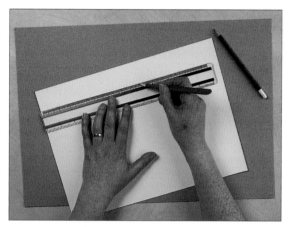

1 Using a pencil, a straight-edge and craft knife, mark and then cut a rectangle from thin card. The corners must be exact right angles or the edges will not come together when folded. The size of the rectangle should be the height of your card and twice its width.

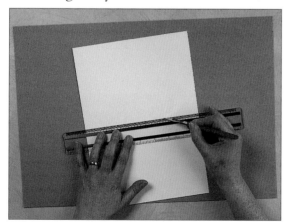

2 Draw a fine pencil line across the middle front of the card. Score the line using the back of the craft knife blade. This will make a sharp indentation but will not cut the card.

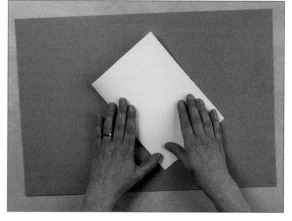

3 With the scored line on the outside, the card will now bend easily in half. Do not put too much pressure on the fold until the card edges have been lined up. Press along the score, and then sharpen the fold with your thumb or a small craft roller.

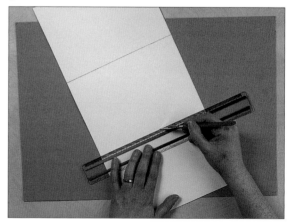

4 A double-folded card has three panels and two scores. Divide the card into three, making one of the outer panels 1mm ($^1/_{16}$in) smaller than the other. Score and fold twice.

Handmade paper

1 Handmade paper (see pages 10–19) can be used to make cards, as long as it is thick enough to stay in shape when decorated, but not so thick that it is difficult to cut or fold. The edges of the paper can be cut using scissors; for a rougher, natural look, draw a faint pencil line, wet the paper, and then tear slowly, working against a ruler. This will give an uneven, torn finish to the edge of the card.

2 Score the paper down through the middle using a ruler and the back of a craft knife. With the scored line on the outside, bend the card in half and press along the score. If you are using dark-coloured paper, use double-sided tape to stick a folded, paper insert inside the card, on which to write your message.

Cutting an aperture

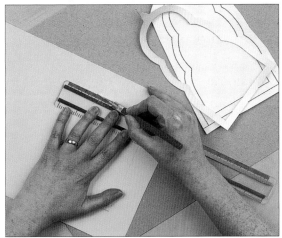

Use a pencil and ruler to mark a window opening on the front flap of your card. Take great care that the window is central, and that all the corners are 90° angles. Cut out the window using a craft knife. For a double folded card with three panels, the window must be in the middle panel.

Adding a decorative panel

An extra layer or panel can be added to the front of a dark or plain card as a base for the decoration. Cut the panel from textured or plain paper or card, fabric, or wide ribbon. Finish the edges of the panel with torn, frayed or decorated edges using deckle-edged scissors. Glue the panel to the card front.

Finishing Techniques

Handmade paper, tin, foam and acetate are just a few of the materials that can be used to decorate cards. When adding 3-D embellishment to the front of a card, remember to get the correct balance or the card will not stand up. If the card is an unusual shape or size you may need to make a special envelope or presentation box

Cutting and painting foam

1 Mark the design directly on to the surface of the foam using a fine marker pen, or make a paper template of the design and draw around it. Lay the foam on to a cutting mat and cut around the design lines using a sharp craft knife.

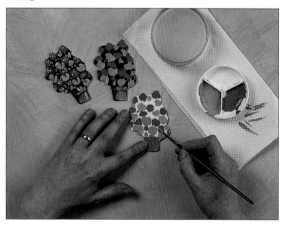

2 Using a small brush, build up the design with several thin layers of acrylic paint. The design can be painted freehand or marked on to the foam using a marker pen.

Cutting and punching tin

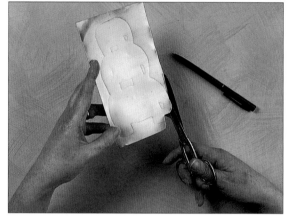

1 Transfer the design on to tin sheeting using a ballpoint pen. Cut around the outer edge of the design using a large pair of scissors. For the smaller cut-away areas use small scissors or a craft knife. Take care not to cut your hands on the sharp metal edges.

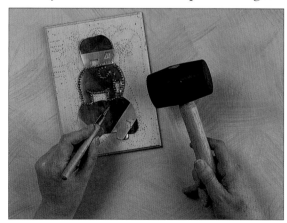

2 Place the metal on to a soft wooden board. Place the tip of the punching tool on the metal and gently hit the tool with the hammer, making a decorative hole in the metal.

Using artificial flowers

Flowers used for decorating cakes, or small silk or paper flowers which are very light-weight, all make good card decorations. The flowers and leaves can be glued individually on to the front of the card, or attached in small bunches, held together with florist's wire, then wrapped in cellophane and ribbon.

Using dried flowers

Small dried flowers, seed heads and lavender can be used to decorate cards. Use flowers that are the correct proportion for the card, cutting them individually from the bunches. Leave a small length of stem on each flower; if a stem is weak or broken, strengthen it with a piece of fine wire.

Using outliner paste

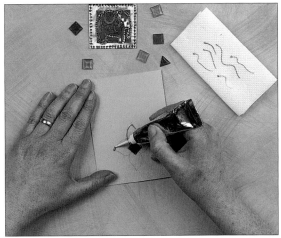

Outliner paste can be used on almost any surface to add detail or to outline objects like jewels, fabric or metal sheeting. Squeeze the tube of outliner paste gently, as if using an icing tube. The spread of the paste will depend on the temperature: warm, dry conditions are best.

Using buttons and beads

Small jewels, beads, buttons, mosaic tiles and old jewellery – a single earring or a backless brooch – can be used to decorate cards, as long as they have one flat side. Glue a piece of torn handmade paper, card or fabric on to the card and then mount the object using tacky glue or a glue gun.

Painting acetate

1 Use thick acetate to make a window in a card or to make a hanging mobile. Use outliner paste to draw the shape on to the surface of the acetate, making sure there are no gaps in the paste, especially at the intersections. Use flexible glass paint in a squeezable tube, which should be applied directly on to the surface of the acetate. Use a cocktail stick to blend the colours together.

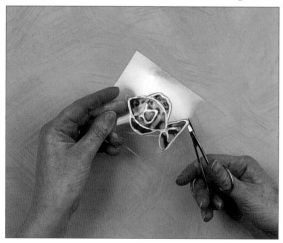

2 Once the paint is dry, cut out the shape just outside the outer paste line. Suspend the painted shape on invisible thread in the window opening of the card. If the acetate has to fit exactly into an opening cut in the card, make it slightly bigger, and then glue it behind the opening, inside the card.

Using glitter glue

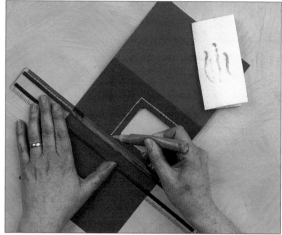

Glitter glue is very easy to use on cards, and comes in gold, silver and a range of bright colours. Shake the tube before you begin, then squeeze it gently on to the card. Use it freehand, against a straight-edge or over a pencil line drawn on the card. Leave the glitter glue to dry overnight.

Drawing an outline

A metallic pen can be used to outline a window opening or to add a border around the outside of the card. Choose a pen with a fine nib; shake the pen well and then make straight, dotted or dashed lines on the card. Work freehand, over a pencil line or against a ruler or straight-edge.

Making Card Accessories

To make a handmade card into an extra-special gift, add a matching tag and decorated envelope. Finish the tag in the same material and colour as the card; the envelope can be decorated with a metallic pen and outliner paste, with a smaller version of the card design attached to the front or the back flap

Making gift tags

1 Cut a tag from the same paper as you are using for the card. Copy an area of the card design that fits on to the tag or, using a larger part of the design, make a tracing, and then reduce its size on a photocopier. Punch one or two holes on one side of the tag.

2 Decorate the tag using the same material as the card. Thread the tag with a length of raffia, string, thread or ribbon, then finish the ends with a bow or knot.

Making an envelope

1 Lay the card down on to thick, coloured paper. Draw a rectangle on to the paper, using a pencil and ruler, slightly larger than the card, then add flaps to the four edges. Score along each side of the rectangle using a ruler and the back of a craft knife.

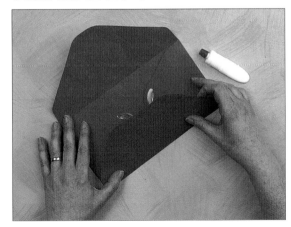

2 Fold the side flaps in, and the bottom flap up, and glue these three flaps together using tacky glue. The envelope can now be decorated to match the card.

Papier Mâché

TOOLS, MATERIALS AND TECHNIQUES

Essential equipment

Below is a list of equipment needed when working with papier mâché:

- **Mixing bowl**: used for mixing paper pulp
- **Strainer or sieve**: used to strain excess water from paper pulp
- **Liquidizer or blender**: used for breaking paper down into pulp
- **Strong plastic bag**: used for mixing ready-mixed paper pulp
- **Clingfilm**: used for wrapping around a mould before adding the pulp
- **Paper**: use copier paper to make a tracing of the design
- **Decorator's paintbrush**: used for applying varnish
- **Paintbrush**: used for applying PVA to newspaper pieces
- **Newspaper**: used for covering your work surface
- **Kitchen paper**: for cleaning equipment
- **Rubber gloves**: to protect your hands when colouring paper pulp with dye
- **Soft cloth and spoon**: for pressing paper pulp into a mould
- **Cutting knife**: used for cutting a cardboard framework for making trays and boxes
- **Masking tape**: used for joining cardboard
- **Sandpaper**: used for rubbing down the surface of papier mâché
- **Jam jar**: used for storing dilute PVA

Making paper pulp

Below is a list of consumables that you will need when making pulp:

- **Cartridge paper**: white or coloured can be used to make paper pulp
- **Brown paper, sugar paper, handmade paper and newspaper**: any decorative or coloured paper that will break down when soaked overnight in water can also be used

- **Ready-mixed paper pulp**: white or off-white substance that is mixed with water to make pulp. Bought from craft shops, as a fine powder or a more fibrous mix; blend with water and a little washing-up liquid for a user-friendly pulp
- **PVA glue**: mix with the sieved pulp in the proportions of approximately 15g (1/2oz) glue to 250g (1/2lb) pulp
- **Washing-up liquid**: blend with pulp for a more malleable mix
- **Water**: soak the paper overnight in water, then add more water to the mix before blending into a pulp
- **Cold water fabric dye**: used to colour pulp

Layered papier mâché

Below is a list of consumables that you will need for applying paper strips:

- **Newspaper**: although other fine paper can be used, newspaper makes the best layered papier mâché

- **PVA glue**: paste the strips of newspaper using a mix of 3 parts PVA to 1 part water
- **Petroleum jelly**: rub over the mould to stop the paper layers sticking to it

Useful hints and tips

- ✔ Add plenty of water when blending pulp
- ✔ It is easier to make it in small quantities
- ✔ Remove excess water from the prepared pulp
- ✔ Use your hands to mix in the PVA
- ✔ Adding washing-up liquid to ready-mixed pulp will make it more malleable
- ✔ Mixed paper pulp can be kept in the refrigerator if sealed in a plastic bag
- ✔ Use plenty of PVA when pasting paper layers
- ✔ Brush out air bubbles under the layers

Painting papier mâché

- ✔ Prime papier mâché with white emulsion or acrylic gesso before painting
- ✔ Use emulsion, acrylic, gouache, powder or metallic paint
- ✔ Seal with matt or gloss acrylic varnish

Which mould?

Almost anything can be used as a mould when making papier mâché, but remember to use a barrier to stop the paper sticking to the mould. Below are some of the points to consider when choosing the right mould to work with.

- **China or plastic bowls and platters**
  - Used for making bowl shapes and plates
  - Almost any item can be used as a mould
  - Use with pulp or paper strips
  - Cover with petroleum jelly and clingfilm before applying the pulp
  - Spread with petroleum jelly if using paper strips
  - Build up at least 15 layers of paper strips
- **Card, mounting board and corrugated**
  - Used for constructing boxes and trays
  - Use masking tape to reinforce the joins and for piecing the cardboard together
  - Cover with pasted paper, building up the layers over the cardboard
- **Aluminium foil**
  - Scrunch up to make a core for a ball or cone shape
  - Cover with PVA before adding pulp or paper layers
  - Can be sanded for a smooth finish
- **Fruit and vegetables**
  - Use real fruit and vegetables as a mould to make fake fruit shapes and caskets
  - Cover with petroleum jelly before adding at least 10 layers of paper
  - The paper fruit has to be cut in half to remove the real fruit
  - Can be sanded until smooth
- **Lampshade**
  - Use as a mould when making a conical-shaped vase
  - The metal frame needs to be removed
  - The shade will form part of the finished structure
  - Apply at least 10 layers of paper
- **Balloon**
  - Makes a very good bowl shape
  - Build up at least 15 layers of paper

Making Paper Pulp

Paper is the essential ingredient for papier mâché; you can make it from plain white cartridge paper or you can use newspaper, brown paper, sugar paper or handmade textured paper for interesting effects. If you would rather not make your own pulp, ready-mixed dry paper pulp is easy to use and available at most good craft shops

Handmade pulp

1 Tear paper into narrow strips and then into pieces of about 2.5cm (1in) square, then leave to soak overnight in a bowl of water. Any paper that will break down when left to soak overnight in water can be used for making pulp.

2 Add plenty of water to the mix, then use a hand blender or liquidizer to break down the paper into pulp. It will make it easier if you work with small quantities of pulp.

3 Strain the prepared pulp over a bowl to remove the excess water, then press the water from the pulp using a spoon, or use your hand to squeeze out the remaining water. The pulp should resemble a damp spongy mass when ready.

4 Mix PVA glue with the sieved pulp using your hands, in the proportions of approximately 15g (½oz) glue to 250g (½lb) pulp. The mixture is now ready to use.

Ready-mixed pulp

1 Paper pulp can be bought from most craft shops, as a fine powder or as a more fibrous mix, ready to be mixed with water. Read the instructions on the pack to find out the correct quantities of pulp to water; glue should not be added unless this is stated on the packet. Place the pulp in a strong plastic bag, then add the water: warm water will help to speed up the mixing process.

2 Add a small amount of washing-up liquid to the pulp/water mix. This will make the pulp more malleable and therefore easier to use. Tie a knot in the bag, then knead the mixture thoroughly until all the powder has disappeared and the pulp is smooth and creamy in consistency.

Dyed paper pulp

To colour prepared pulp, make up cold water fabric dye, following the manufacturers' instructions. Add a few drops of dye to the pulp, then leave for several hours before squeezing out the excess. Water-soluble paint can also be used to dye the pulp, but the colours will be less intense.

Coloured paper pulp

Coloured cartridge paper, sugar paper, brown paper and newsprint can also be used to make paper pulp. It should be treated in the same way as white paper: tearing, then soaking in water, before straining, blending and mixing with PVA glue. When dry it will not be as strong in colour as dyed pulp.

Using Paper Pulp

Moulded pulp gives a very different texture to laid paper strips: it is rough in appearance but has a naive charm that is very difficult to achieve in any other medium. Once the coloured or white paper has been made into pulp it can be moulded over or in almost any container, from a serving bowl to a sweet mould.

Moulding over a container

1 Here a bowl is used as a mould, although almost any container is suitable. Grease the mould with petroleum jelly, then wrap in clingfilm. Place lumps of prepared white or coloured papier mâché pulp firmly on to the mould, making a thin even layer.

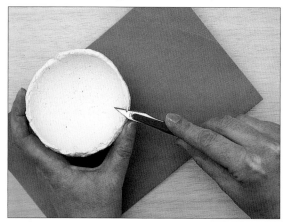

2 When the pulp is dry, ease the paper bowl from the mould, and peel off the clingfilm. Use a sharp knife to tidy the top of the bowl, then finish with sandpaper.

3 Before painting, a white paper bowl should be primed with two coats of white emulsion or acrylic gesso: this will give a good basecoat for the paint. Decorate the bowl with acrylic paint, then finish with two coats of gloss or matt acrylic varnish.

4 Paper pulp can also be moulded inside a bowl. Grease with petroleum jelly, then wrap in clingfilm before pressing the pulp well down into the bowl with a spoon.

Using plastic sweet moulds

1 Brush neat washing-up liquid over the inside of each mould, getting it well down into the corners. Press a small amount of prepared paper pulp into the mould; turn the mould over and check there are no air bubbles in the pulp, then fill until level with the top. When dry, the paper shapes will shrink away from the sides of the mould and can then be easily tipped out.

2 Using sharp scissors, cut away any excess paper that surrounds the paper shapes, then finish the edges with fine sandpaper. Prime the shapes with white emulsion or gesso before decorating with acrylic paint. Lastly, seal the surface with a coat of gloss or matt acrylic varnish.

Using aluminium foil

Aluminium foil can be used to make shapes, like balls and cones, because of the lightness of the material. A coat of dilute PVA glue on the foil will help the papier mâché pulp to stick; press the pulp on to the wet glue, moulding it well in place. When the pulp is dry it can be sanded and painted.

Using a template

A template can be placed under clingfilm as a guide for making coloured shapes in a moulded bowl. Attach the templates with double-sided tape, then rub the bowl with petroleum jelly before wrapping in clingfilm. Work the patterned areas first, then fill in around them, moulding the colours together.

Using Paper Strips

Almost anything can be used as a mould for newspaper strips as long as it is covered with clingfilm and/or petroleum jelly to stop the paper sticking to it. Use dilute PVA glue to apply the newspaper; the smaller the strips, and the more layers you apply, the better the finished effect will be

Pasting over a dish

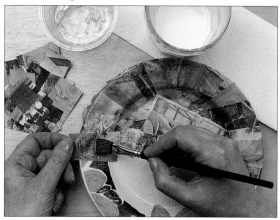

Rub petroleum jelly over the surface of a plate. Paste on strips of newspaper using a mix of 3 parts PVA to 1 part water; apply 15 layers. Leave to dry, then ease from the plate.

Pasting over fruit

Rub petroleum jelly over the surface of a fruit or vegetable, then paste layers of newspaper over the surface. When dry, cut in half and remove the fruit or vegetable in one piece.

Pasting over a lampshade

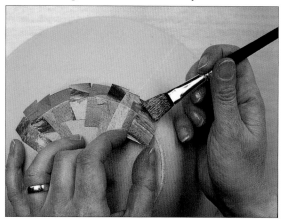

To make a conical-shaped bowl: remove the fittings from inside a lampshade, then stick a card circle over one end. Paste newspaper strips over the surface, building up the layers.

Using coloured paper

Coloured paper can be used instead of paint to decorate papier mâché. When the newspaper is dry, apply a final layer of gift-wrap or tissue-paper strips using diluted PVA glue.

Pasting over a balloon

1 A quick and easy way to make a footed bowl is to use a balloon as a mould. To make the bowl base, tape a strip of cardboard into a ring, then cover the bottom with a card circle. Paste strips of newspaper so that they overlap the join between the ring and the base circle, using diluted PVA glue; leave to dry. Blow up a balloon and sit it, smaller end down, into a flower pot.

2 Place the base on top of the balloon. Apply five layers of newspaper strips to the base and top third of the balloon; leave to dry. Pop the balloon and remove it from the paper bowl. Using sharp scissors cut the upper edge of the bowl level. Prime with white emulsion or gesso, then decorate.

Pasting over cardboard

1 Build your tray or box shape from corrugated cardboard, held together with pieces of masking tape. Use a cutting board and sharp knife to cut the card, making sure the pieces are exactly the right size or they will not fit perfectly together. Fit the shorter sides, then the longer, overlapping the base and shorter sides. Use masking tape on the edges to keep the sides square.

2 Paste small strips of newspaper over the joins and the corners of the cardboard using dilute PVA glue. Smooth the pieces down, removing all air bubbles. Build up the layers over the cardboard, overlapping the edges of the paper: each layer should be laid in a different direction for strength.

Stamping

TOOLS, MATERIALS AND TECHNIQUES

Essential equipment

Below is a list of the equipment needed when stamping:

- **Paper:** use copier paper to make a tracing of the design
- **Cutting mat:** a mat that self-heals when cut and will protect your work surface
- **Cutting knife:** slim craft knife, sharp enough to carve sponge or foam and to cut rubber erasers, cork and polystyrene tiles
- **Artist's paintbrush:** used to coat the surface of a stamp with paint
- **Decorator's paintbrush:** used to apply a wash, base coat or varnish to wood
- **Foam roller:** used for rolling paint on to the surface of a stamp
- **Paint dish:** flat plastic microwave dish or fresh food tray
- **Kitchen paper:** useful for mopping up spills and for cleaning stamps
- **Cotton buds:** used to clean stamps
- **Cotton wool:** used to clean stamps
- **Cocktail stick:** used for mixing paint
- **Fine sandpaper:** used for rubbing down wooden surfaces before stamping
- **Toaster:** for melting embossing powder when applied to paper
- **Masking tape:** use strips as a guide for stamping
- **Corrugated card:** a base for mounting cork, polystyrene, string and leaves
- **Wooden blocks:** a base for mounting foam sheet or string shapes

Tips for stamping on paper

- ✔ Do not overload the paper with paint
- ✔ Leave the stamped paper to dry flat
- ✔ Use acrylic and emulsion paint on paper
- ✔ Add detail to a stamped image with a thick-nibbed, felt-tipped pen
- ✔ Stamp lining paper to make inexpensive gift-wrap
- ✔ Use embossing ink and powder to add an extra dimension to paper

Tips for stamping on fabric

- ✔ Wash to remove 'finishing' and shrinkage
- ✔ Test the paint on the fabric, for bleeding
- ✔ Fix fabric paint with an iron after stamping
- ✔ Cover fabric that you are not working on with paper, to keep it clean

- ✔ Stick masking tape strips or lengths of lining paper to the fabric to use as guides
- ✔ Some fabric paint will be too thin for stamping: add stencil paint to thicken it

Making stamps

Below is a list of items from which you can make stamps:

- **Cork floor tiles**: thin floor tile made from closely packed cork
- **Washing-up sponge**: use a firm sponge or kitchen scourer
- **Packing foam**: a sheet of white foam
- **Potato**: half a large, raw baking potato
- **Rubber eraser**: pre-shaped rubbers or stamps cut from rubber erasers
- **Wooden clothes peg**: remove the metal spring from a clothes peg, then use the flat wooden end as a stamp

- **Fruit**: any firm-skinned fruit or vegetable with an interesting internal structure
- **Leaves**: fresh green leaves with pronounced veins
- **Plastic cotton reels**: use the spokes at the end of a cotton reel to stamp wheels on vehicles
- **String**: stick coiled string to cardboard
- **Corks**: use wine bottle corks
- **Hands**: dip your hands in paint, then walk them across the project surface
- **Foam-rubber block**: carve stamps from tightly packed high-density foam
- **Polystyrene tile**: cut shapes from ceiling tiles then stick to mount board

Choosing the right paint

Choosing the right paint for the right surface can be difficult: listed below are some of the plus and minus points to help you decide.

- **Acrylic: water-based**
  The right consistency for stamping
  Colours can be mixed
  Large range of colours available
  Will give good results on most surfaces
  Brushes can be washed in water
  Dries fast
  Use water-based varnish to seal
- **Emulsion: water-based**
  Sold in small tester pots
  Mostly pale colours, but can be mixed
  Use as a base coat to stamp on to
- **Ceramic: water-based**
  Use on china, ceramics and tiles
  Will air-dry in 72 hours
  High gloss finish
  Can be used on bathroom tiles
  Most are dishwasher safe on china
- **Fabric paint: water-based**
  Some makes are too thin for stamping
  Colours can be mixed
  Test for 'bleeding'
  Brushes can be washed in water
  Iron fix before laundering
- **Matt acrylic varnish: water-based**
  Brush- and spray-on
  Wash brushes in water
  No smell and dries very quickly
- **Polyurethane varnish: oil-based**
  Brush-on, very slow to dry
  Wash brushes in white spirit
  Work in a well ventilated room
  Very tough finish
- **Stamping ink**
  Use an ink pad to load the stamp
  Used mainly with ready-made stamps
  Difficult to clean up spills
- **Embossing ink**
  Use an ink pad to load the stamp
  Glue – not paint or ink
  Used only under embossing powder
  Holds powder to project until melted

Making Stamps

Almost any object with one flat surface can be used to make a stamp. It must have an interesting shape, surface or internal structure, and be able to transfer paint to the project surface. Stamps need not be expensive: organic material like fruit and leaves can make some very interesting stamped shapes

Using corks & clothes pegs

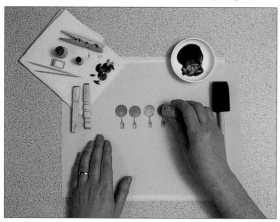

The end of a wooden clothes peg will make a rectangular shape, whereas a cork makes a mottled circle. You could try combining the two shapes to make an interesting design.

Using string

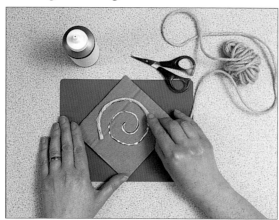

Draw spirals and coils on to corrugated card. Glue along the drawn lines, then lay string over the glue. Cut off the excess string. Trim the card just larger than the string shape.

Using rubber erasers

Stamp with pre-shaped rubbers or cut your own design from a rubber eraser: attach a paper pattern to the rubber, then cut around the edge using a sharp craft knife.

Using foam-rubber block

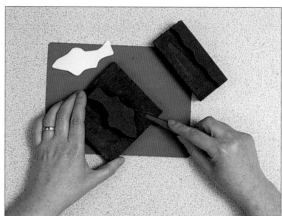

High-density foam-rubber block makes a good stamp. Make a tracing of the design, then pin to the foam. Cut away the excess foam, leaving the design as a raised block.

Using leaves

Place a leaf on to mount board or card. Then use a ballpoint pen to trace around the leaf. Cut out the shape inside the drawn lines, so that the card is very slightly smaller than the leaf. Glue the top side of the leaf to the card shape, then glue a small piece of mount board to the card to act as a handle.

Using potatoes

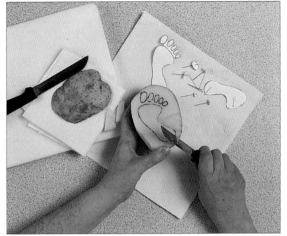

Cut a large firm baking potato in half lengthways. Dry the cut surface, then place on kitchen paper to soak up any excess fluid. Pin a design tracing to the surface of the potato, then draw around it with felt-tipped pen. Cut away the potato outside the drawn lines, to a depth of 1cm (3/8in).

Using your hands

Place the paint next to the fabric, and have kitchen paper handy so that you can wipe your hands easily. Place your hand in the paint, making sure that every part of it is well covered: use a brush to add more paint if needed. Press your hand firmly on the fabric, then remove carefully.

Using sponge

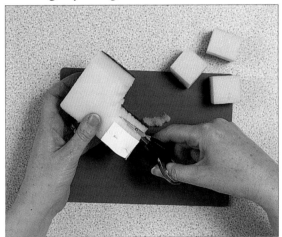

Make a paper template of the design, then pin the template to the top of a washing-up sponge. Using sharp scissors, carefully cut the sponge to the same size as the template. The sponge will soak up the paint making it difficult to clean, so make a stamp for each paint colour used.

Using a cotton reel

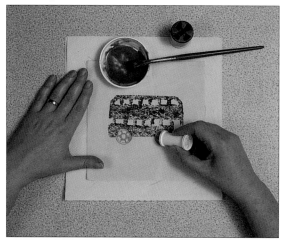

To make wheels on a stamped vehicle, use the end of a cotton reel: remove the paper circle from the end of a plastic cotton reel to reveal the 'spokes'. Apply paint to the spokes, using a paintbrush. Gently press the cotton reel on to the stamped vehicle. Re-apply the paint before stamping again.

Using fruit

Using a sharp knife and working on a clean chopping board, cut a piece of fruit in half then lay it cut side down on kitchen paper to absorb the juice. Use a paint brush or roller to coat the fruit with paint. Firm-skinned fruits or vegetables, with an interesting internal structure, make the best stamps.

Using cork tiles

Make a paper template of your design, then lay the template on to a cork tile. Draw around the shape with a ballpoint pen, then cut using a sharp craft knife or scissors. Cut a piece of stiff cardboard slightly larger than the cork shape. Using PVA glue, stick the cork shape to its cardboard backing.

Using foam sheet

Lay petal-shaped paper templates on to a sheet of packing foam, and draw around the shapes with a felt-tipped pen. Using craft scissors cut out the foam petals. Sand down the surface of a block of wood, then use craft glue to stick six or eight petals firmly on to the top of the block, forming a circle.

Stamping Techniques

Stamping is just a matter of transferring paint or ink to the project surface, but how you load the paint and how much you use will change the look of the stamped image. Too much paint and the image will fill in, too little and it will be broken. Here we help you find the right method

Loading the stamp pad

Stamping or embossing ink should be applied to a stamp from a pad. Spread the ink over the pad using a sponge brush: allow the ink to soak into the pad before using.

Loading the stamp

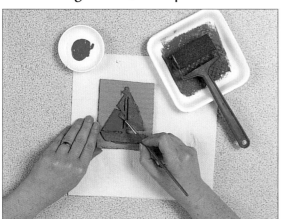

Use a brush to apply paint to the surface of a stamp; if you are using the stamp repeatedly, a roller will be quicker to use and gives a very even paint application.

Embossing

1 Load an ink pad with embossing ink, press the stamp on to the ink, then stamp firmly on to paper. Before the ink dries, sprinkle embossing powder liberally on the ink. Leave for a few seconds then carefully shake off the excess powder.

2 Hold the stamped paper over the top of a heated toaster for a few seconds to melt the embossing powder. Do not overheat the powder, or it will lose its shine.

Hints and Tips

Good preparation is important when stamping, if you want a professional finish. Keeping your equipment and stamps clean will ensure that paint only goes where it's intended – if a spill does occur, then kitchen roll is invaluable for clearing it up

Preparing your work surface

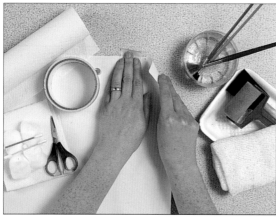

Before you begin stamping, cover your work surface with clean lining paper. Keep all your equipment close at hand, and clean water and kitchen paper to mop up any stray paint.

Working on wood

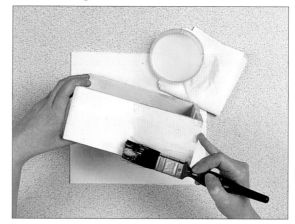

To colour bare wood before stamping, sand the surface of the wood, then wipe with a damp cloth. When dry, paint with several coats of acrylic paint thinned with water.

Preparing for painting

Always prepare surfaces before stamping: use fine sandpaper on wood; scrub terracotta flower pots in warm soapy water; and launder fabric to remove any 'finishing'.

Applying varnish to wood

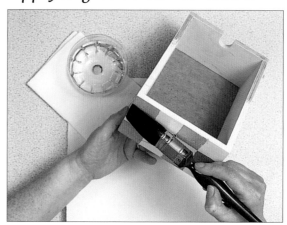

Seal the surface of stamped wood with two coats of matt or satin varnish to protect it from dirty marks. Use acrylic varnish on water-based paint and polyurethane on oil.

Working on fabric

Always test the paint on the fabric before you begin stamping: some will allow the paint to soak in rapidly; others will let it 'bleed' into the weave. Depending on your test, you may need to thin down the paint with a little water, or thicken it with fabric or stencil paint of a similar colour.

Fixing fabric paint

Leave fabric paint to dry, then heat it to fix the paint. Cover the fabric with a cotton cloth, or place it face down on a fluffy towel. Iron for 1–2 minutes on the hottest setting suitable for the fabric. Although most fabric paint is heat-fixed, read the manufacturer's instructions before proceeding.

Working on tiles

Almost any paint can be used on untreated terracotta floor tiles, as long as they are sealed first with emulsion paint; on shiny glazed tiles, use a water-based cold-set ceramic paint. This sort will air-dry in about 72 hours and its high gloss finish is waterproof enough to use in the bathroom.

Cleaning your stamps

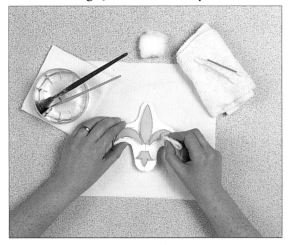

It is important to keep all your equipment clean when stamping. Wipe the stamp between each colour change and at regular intervals when in use. On water-based paints, use cotton wool or a cotton bud dipped in water; on oil paints use white spirit. Dry the stamp thoroughly before re-using.

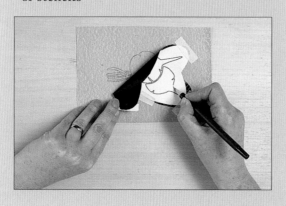

Stencilling
TOOLS, MATERIALS AND TECHNIQUES

Essential equipment

Below is a list of the essential equipment needed to cut stencils:

- **Stencil card**: thick yellow card, soaked in linseed oil to make it waterproof and pliable
- **Acetate and stencil film**: a pliable clear plastic on to which the design can be drawn, and through which it will show from below
- **Cork**: pliable thin cork or a cork tile; good for stencilling on fabric
- **Paper**: use copier paper to trace or photocopy the design. Useful when making masks for reverse stencilling
- **Typewriter carbon paper**: use this for transferring a tracing to stencil card
- **Cutting mat**: a mat that self-heals when cut and will protect your work surface
- **Cutting knife**: slim, very sharp craft knife used for cutting stencil card or acetate
- **Fine sandpaper**: use decorator's sandpaper for rubbing down wooden surfaces, and removing snags from the underside of stencils

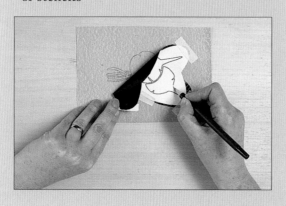

Painting with stencils

Below is a list of the essential equipment needed for painting stencil designs:

- **Stencil brush**: a stiff bristled brush with a flat top, made in different sizes and thicknesses
- **Sponge**: use a natural sea sponge for a soft paint effect, or a synthetic spong cut from a kitchen scourer for a more textured effect
- **Artist's paintbrush**: use to add highlights to a wet or dry stencilled design or to add fine lines to flower stems or leaf veins
- **Decorator's paintbrush**: use to apply a wash or base coat to wood or to add a coat of varnish
- **Dish for mixing paint**: use a plastic microwave dish, fresh food tray or tinfoil dish, or a small artist's palette
- **Kitchen paper**: useful for removing excess paint from a brush, mopping up spills and cleaning brushes
- **Cotton buds**: used to clean stencils
- **Cocktail stick**: used for mixing paint

Tips for stencilling on tiles

- ✔ Use terracotta or unsealed floor tiles
- ✔ Seal the surface with matt emulsion paint
- ✔ Use acrylic paints, as they have the brightest colour range
- ✔ Apply the paint using a sponge
- ✔ Seal the stencilled tile with acrylic varnish
- ✔ Only use stencilled tiles in low wear areas

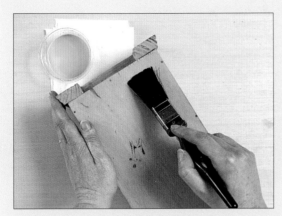

Tips for stencilling on wood

✔ Rub down the wood using fine sandpaper
✔ Colour the surface of bare wood with a wash
✔ Use spray adhesive to mount the stencil
✔ Seal the stencilled wood with acrylic varnish

Tips for stencilling on metal

✔ Rub down with wet and dry sandpaper
✔ Use a spray primer to seal the bare metal
✔ Allow to dry before removing the stencil
✔ Seal the surface with polyurethane varnish

Tips for stencilling on paper

✔ Use uncoated paper
✔ Do not overload the paper with paint
✔ Spray paint will give the best finish
✔ Doilies make good masks for stencilling
✔ Leave the stencilled paper to dry flat

Tips for stencilling on fabric

✔ Use calico or cotton-based fabric
✔ Wash to remove 'finishing' and shrinkage
✔ Test the paint on the fabric, for bleeding
✔ Fix fabric paint with an iron before washing
✔ Use fabric paint for most fabrics; emulsion
   paint can be used on stiff fabric like hessian
✔ Seal emulsion with a PVA glue/water mix

Choosing the right paint

Choosing the right paint for the right surface can be difficult: listed below are some of the plus and minus points to help you decide.

● **Stencil paint: water-based**
  The right consistency for stencilling
  Colours can be mixed
  Will give good results on most surfaces
  Brushes can be washed in water
  Use water-based varnish to seal
  Very expensive compared with acrylics

● **Acrylic: water-based**
  The right consistency for stencilling
  Large range of colours available (can be mixed)
  Will give good results on most surfaces
  Brushes can be washed in water
  Dries fast, may need a 'retarder'
  Use water-based varnish to seal

● **Emulsion: water-based**
  Sold in small tester pots
  Mostly pale colours, but can be mixed
  Too slow to dry for most projects
  Paint thin, but works well on fabric

● **Fabric paint: water-based**
  Some makes too thin for stencilling
  Colours can be mixed
  Test for 'bleeding'
  Brushes can be washed in water
  Iron-fix before laundering

● **Enamel paint: oil-based**
  Use on metal surfaces
  Brushes must be cleaned in white spirit
  Work in a well ventilated room

● **Spray paint: most are cellulose-based**
  Must be stored at room temperature
  Use in a well ventilated room
  Shake well, spray from 30–46cm (12–18in)

● **Matt acrylic varnish: water-based**
  Brush and spray-on
  Wash brushes in water
  No smell and dries very quickly

● **Polyurethane varnish: oil-based**
  Brush-on, very slow to dry
  Wash brushes in white spirit
  Work in a well ventilated room

Making Stencils

A stencil can be cut from almost any flat material: card, acetate, clear film, cork or paper. How you make a stencil and what you make it from depends on the craft materials that are available to you. Each of the stencil projects recommends a method of working, but you may prefer to try a different technique

Using carbon paper

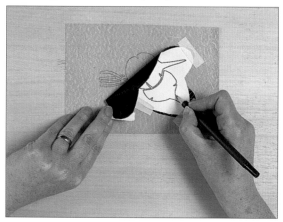

To transfer the design to stencil card, place typewriter carbon paper between the card and the tracing. Draw over the lines firmly using a ballpoint pen.

Cutting out the stencil

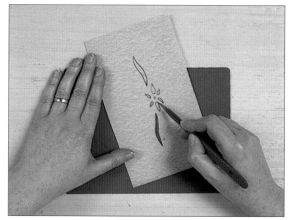

Hold the uncut stencil on a cutting mat and, following the design lines, start cutting from the centre. Move the stencil as you cut, drawing the knife towards you.

Using acetate

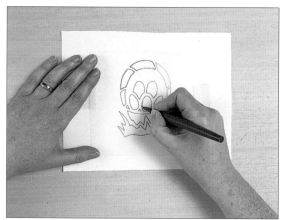

To transfer the design to clear acetate or stencil film, place a tracing of the design under the acetate or film then draw over the lines firmly using a felt-tipped pen.

Rubbing down

After cutting the stencil, check the underside for snags – these should be removed, using fine sandpaper, to ensure the stencil will fit snugly when attached to the prepared surface.

Mounting a stencil

Lay the stencil face down on paper. Working in a well ventilated room, coat the back with spray mount adhesive – this will keep the stencil flat while painting, but can easily be removed with white spirit. Position the stencil on the prepared painting surface, holding in place with masking tape.

Repairing a stencil

To repair a stencil if you make a mistake whilst cutting or it gets broken while in use, clean around the area to be mended, then lay the stencil on a cutting mat covering the break with sticky tape. Turn the stencil over and repeat on the other side. Cut away the excess tape using a sharp craft knife.

Making a leaf stencil

To make a stencil from a leaf or flat object: attach the leaf or object to a thin cork sheet using sticky tape. Draw around the shape with a felt-tipped pen. Place the cork on a cutting mat and, using a sharp craft knife or small scissors, cut around the drawn shape, neatening any points or corners.

Using a cookie cutter

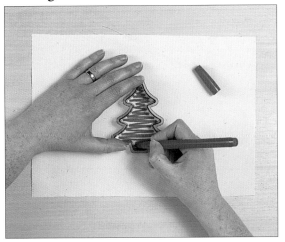

To scribble-stencil on to fabric, position a cookie cutter on to the prepared fabric, holding firmly with one hand. Using a fabric-painting felt pen and starting at the top, scribble from side to side within the cutter, touching each side as you move down towards the bottom of the shape.

Painting Techniques

Traditionally stencil paint is applied using a flat-ended brush, but you may want to try another method of applying the paint. A sponge dipped in paint and dabbed on to the surface will give a mottled folk art look, or you could try using spray paint to give a finer, more even paint finish

Loading the brush

Load the stencil brush with paint, then dab on to kitchen paper to remove the excess paint, giving an almost dry brush. Do this each time you add paint to the brush.

Adding highlights

To highlight the design use a small stencil brush to dab paint on to the wet or dry stencilled design, at the edges or the centre to give a three-dimensional effect.

Pouncing

Using a loaded stencil brush, apply paint to the parts of the design not covered by the stencil. Use a soft pouncing or gentle circular movement with the brush.

Sponging

Dip a piece of sponge into the paint. Dab the sponge on to the design area not covered by the stencil. Apply the paint lightly to create a mottled effect.

Using a doily

In a well ventilated room, lightly coat the back of a doily with spray adhesive, then position it right side up on a sheet of paper. Shake the paint can, then holding upright, spray the doily and the paper between, from a distance of 30–46cm (12–18in). Remove the doily, leave to dry.

Cleaning a stencil

Keep the stencil free from paint by cleaning both sides between applications. Use kitchen paper and a cotton bud dipped in water to remove water-based paint; for oil- based paint, use white spirit. Good adhesion to the working surface will stop the paint 'bleeding' behind the stencil.

Reverse stencilling on fabric

Stretch the material on to card, then mask off the areas not to be painted – use paper shapes attached with tape or torn masking tape strips. Using a large stencil brush, dab fabric paint on to the material, building up the colour slowly. Leave to dry, then remove the paper shapes. To fix the paint, see page 58.

Washing brushes

Wash brushes in warm soapy water at regular intervals while in use, and when changing paint colour – this will stop a build-up of paint. Clean and dry the brushes thoroughly before storing upright. A rubber band wrapped around the bristles will help keep them in good condition.

Painting on Fabric

Stencilling on fabric requires extra care in preparation and finishing. Many fabrics need to be washed first to remove any finishes and ensure no further shrinkage will take place. For fabric that cannot be laundered, coat with a mix of PVA glue and water. This will seal the surface, protecting it from dirt

Preparing fabric

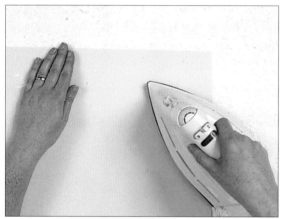

Fabric should be laundered before applying paint to remove the 'finishing' and take up any shrinkage in the fabric: wash in warm soapy water, then iron on a fluffy towel.

Fixing fabric paint

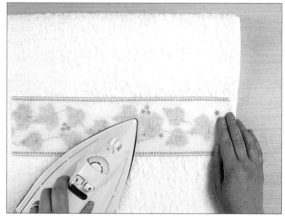

Stencilled fabric should be heat-fixed to stop the paint washing out. Place the dry fabric face down on a towel. Iron for 1–2 minutes on the hottest setting suitable for the fabric.

Using fabric paint

Working with an almost dry brush, pounce paint within the design area of the stencil. Remove the stencil, clean, then reposition on the fabric. To fix the paint, see above.

Sealing surfaces

To protect fabric that is difficult to launder, coat with PVA glue mixed with an equal quantity of water, working the mix into the weave of the fabric. Dry flat for several days.

Hints and Tips

Some surfaces will require a little more preparation work than others. If you are working on wood, you may want to colour the background; on tiles the surface will need sealing. Here you will find useful advice that will speed up the work, leaving more time for the stencilling

Masking tape guides

When stencilling in rows on fabric, make a paper marker that is just larger than the width of the design. Use pins to mark rows across the fabric. Stick masking tape along the rows.

Applying a wash to wood

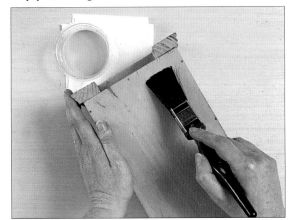

To colour a wooden surface before stencilling, lightly sand the wood, then wipe with a damp cloth. Mix emulsion paint with water, then paint the wood, leaving to dry overnight.

Covering a mistake

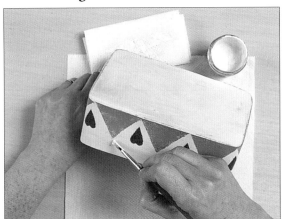

To remove stencil paint that has spread on to the background, sand the mark carefully, then wipe clean using a damp cloth. Repaint the area with the background colour.

Stencilling on tiles

Paint quarry or unsealed tiles with three coats of emulsion paint, before you begin stencilling. After stencilling, seal the tile with several coats of matt acrylic varnish.

GREETINGS CARDS

Almost every occasion of the year can be marked with a special greetings card, whether it is to mark a birthday or anniversary, to wish good luck, or even just to say 'hello'. So why not add a special touch and send a handmade card? Take a look at these exciting ideas and make a card that is as special and as individual as the recipient.

★ **Bright Daisy Cards** (page 62) are made from corrugated card decorated with foam pieces to create a variety of colour and texture.

★ **Miniature Scrap Ideas** (page 66) offers ten quick and easy ideas for making cards from all kinds of bits and pieces.

★ **3-D Greetings** (page 70) combines stamping and 3-D découpage to create designs to embellish all kinds of cards and gifts.

★ **Glittering Christmas Cards** (page 74) use recycled napkins and tinsel to give them a real festive feel. Additional ideas for matching gift presentation means you'll have Christmas all wrapped up!

★ **Organic Nature Cards** (page 78) make the most of organic colours and textures, embellished with natural materials such as bark, twigs, dried flowers and hessian.

★ **Moon and Star Cards** (page 84) will thrill anyone who loves the night sky, with their inky blue background, twinkling highlights and range of shining metallic finishes.

★ **Notes from the Garden** (page 88) brings outdoors in, with dried flowers and other garden finds used to fill the terracotta pots on the front of these charming little houses.

Bright Daisy Cards

These bright, cheery, all-occasion cards are fun and easy to make. The pots of flowers have been cut from thin foam sheeting, which has then been mounted on to coloured corrugated card. Deckle-edged scissors used on the edges of the foam and card creates a very professional finish. (See Techniques page 28)

You will need

- Corrugated card – red, yellow, purple
- Paper – pink, red
- Thin foam sheeting – yellow, pink, purple, blue, red, orange
- Deckle-edged scissors
- Ribbon – blue, green
- Hole punch
- Craft knife, cutting mat, scissors
- Ruler, ballpoint pen, white paper
- Tacky glue, spray adhesive

Making the tall card

1 Cut a rectangle of yellow corrugated card 21x20cm (8¼x8in) using a craft knife and cutting mat: the corrugations should run parallel with the long edge.

2 Using a straight-edge and the back of a craft knife blade, make a score line midway across the width of the card, using one of the corrugations as a guide. Fold the card in half on the score line, lining up the edges of the card.

3 Cut a rectangle of pink paper 7.5x17cm (3x6¾in) and then decorate the edges using a pair of deckle-edged scissors. Glue the rectangle of paper centrally on to the front of the card using spray adhesive.

4 Make individual tracings of the different pieces that make up the large flower pot on page 65: the pot, diamond decoration, stem, flower and flower centre. Cut out each traced component from white paper.

5 Lay the traced flower on to thin purple foam, and draw round the edge using a ballpoint pen. Cut out the foam flower using a craft knife and cutting mat. Now cut the other shapes from foam: use green for the stem; blue for the vase; and red for the flower centre and the seven red diamonds.

6 Use deckle-edged scissors to cut a strip of orange foam to fit across the top of the pot.

7 Glue the flower, stem and pot face down on to the card, so that the ballpoint pen lines do not show. Glue the flower centre on to the flower and the decoration on to the pot.

Making the square card

1 Use a craft knife and cutting mat to cut a rectangle 30x15cm (12x6in) from purple corrugated card. Score and fold the card in half in the same way as for the rectangular card.

2 Cut a 12x12cm (4³/₄x4³/₄in) square of red paper using deckle-edged scissors. Glue it on to the front of the card using spray adhesive.

3 Make individual tracings of the small flower-pot pieces on the opposite page.

4 Lay the flower on to blue foam and draw round the edge using a ballpoint pen. Cut out the flower using a craft knife and cutting mat. Now draw round and cut out the other shapes in the same way: green foam for the stem and leaves; pink for the flower centre and the six diamonds on the pot; orange for the leaf markings; and yellow for the pot.

5 Use the deckle-edged scissors to cut a purple foam strip to fit across the pot.

6 Glue the flower, stem, leaves and pot face down on to the card, so that the pen lines do not show. Glue the flower centre on to the flower and the decoration on to the pot.

Making the gift tags

1 Make a tracing of the gift tag opposite. Cut one tag from red corrugated card, and one from yellow. Use a hole punch to make a hole in the pointed end of each tag.

2 Make a tracing of the two single flowers, and the flower centres, on the opposite page.

3 Cut one flower from yellow foam and the other from pink. The round centres should be cut from blue and orange foam. Glue the flowers and flower centres on to the tags.

4 Cut two lengths of ribbon 24cm (9¹/₂in) long, one in green and one in blue. Thread the ribbon through the holes in the tags.

Large Flower Pot

Small Flower Pot

Flower for Tag

Diamond for Pot
Decoration

Tag

Use these shapes to decorate
your cards. Make tracings of the
individual parts and then cut
them from coloured foam. Cut
the tag from corrugated card.

Miniature Scrap Ideas

You can make miniature cards using almost any small objects or scraps of fabric.
Experiment with using materials in new and interesting ways, combining different
textures and colours. Raid the cupboard for a single button, an odd earring or a scrap
of favourite fabric – the only limit is your imagination! (See Techniques page 28)

You will need

- Craft paper – a selection of colours
- Card – a selection of colours
- Paper – handmade, wrapping, fluorescent
- Corrugated card
- Sheet of gold paper with punched-out stars
- Cork sheeting – thin
- Small objects – dried flowers, odd earrings,
  wooden shapes, beads, buttons, mosaic tiles,
  shells, stones
- Fabric – small-patterned
- Coloured ribbon, coloured string
- Needle and thread – gold
- Metallic pen – gold
- Deckle-edged scissors, ballpoint pen, white
  paper
- Pencil, ruler, craft knife, cutting mat
- Thin wadding

Making cards

1 Draw a 18x18cm (7x7in) square on to
coloured craft paper. Cut out the square using
a craft knife, ruler and cutting mat.

2 Fold the paper in half, lining up the edges
exactly before pressing along the folded
edge. Fold the card in half again, lining up the
edges before pressing along the folded edge.

Making window cards

1 Make a tracing of the rectangular or arch-
shaped window frame on page 69 on to
white paper, and then cut out the frame and
the opening making a complete window-shaped
template. Lay the template on to coloured card
and draw around the outer and inner edges.

2 Choose a piece of patterned fabric and cut it
to fit behind the window opening. Glue the
fabric on to the back of the window frame. Cut
a piece of thin wadding to the same size as the
window opening. Place the wadding behind
the opening, then glue the frame to the card
so that the wadding and the fabric edges are
sandwiched between the frame and the card.

Tearing handmade paper

1 When using handmade paper to make these
miniature cards, all the edges of the paper
should be torn and not cut to give a natural
look. Fold the handmade paper where you want

the tear to be and then dampen with water. Tear the paper slowly along the fold: this will give a very rough edge. For a slightly neater finish, hold a straight-edge lightly on the fold, then tear along it, using the ruler as a guide (see Handmade Paper Card, page 31).

Using a metallic pen

1 Before drawing lines on to the front of your card, you must first check that the ink from your pen will not spread when applied to the surface of the paper. Practise drawing lines on a scrap of the same paper you will be using for the card. The lines can be straight, dashed, dotted or drawn freehand. If you are using a ruler, make sure that it is turned on to its concave side, or the ink may smudge when the pen is pressed against the edge of the ruler.

Decorating the cards

1 Tear a rectangle of brown wrapping paper 6x6cm (2½x2½in) and glue it diagonally on to the front of a blue card. Then tear a rectangle of green handmade paper 4x4cm (1½x1½in), and glue it to the centre of the brown paper. Next, glue

an odd single earring, jewel or a flat metal object to the centre of the card.

2 Use deckle-edged scissors to cut four 7.5cm (3in) strips from the edge of a piece of thin cork sheeting: this makes strips with one straight edge and one patterned. Glue the strips around the edge of a brown card to make a frame. From a sheet of punched gold stars, cut small triangles to fit each corner, then glue them in place. Use the deckle-edged scissors to cut a 3x3cm (1¼x1¼in) square from the cork sheeting. Glue this diagonally on to the centre of the card. Cut a square of punched gold stars slightly smaller than the cork, then glue it in place. Glue a cream fish-shaped button or other object on to the centre of the card.

3 Make a black window frame, with four small panes. Draw gold pen lines around each pane, and around the outer edge of the frame. Glue fabric with a small pattern on to the reverse side of the frame. Glue the frame on to the middle of a red card.

4 Using the outline on the opposite page, make a church window frame from mauve paper. Select a piece of black and gold star fabric, and place it behind the opening in the frame. Cut a piece of wadding the same size as the hole cut in the frame, and place it on the back of the fabric. Glue the frame in the bottom left corner of the card. Thread a large-eyed needle with gold embroidery thread, then tie a knot in the end of the thread. Make long, straight stitches from the points and centre of a star, radiating outwards on to the card. Finish the stitching at the back with a knot and a dab of glue.

5 Glue a 6x6cm (2½x2½in) square of shocking pink card on to a blue card. Glue a small wooden heart, painted with a wash of acrylic paint, on to the centre of the card. Glue twigs or stiff raffia in a square around the heart.

6 Glue a 6x6cm (2½x2½in) square of torn cream handmade paper on to a light sea green card. Then cut a length of green gardening string so that it fits just inside the edges of the cream paper. Tie the ends in a bow and glue the string to the front of the card. Glue a colour-washed wooden shape to the centre of the card.

7 Choose wrapping paper with small individual images and areas that can be used as a border. Cut four strips of the paper for the card edges with mitred 45 degree corners. Then glue the border pieces around the edge of a brown card. Cut out a small image from the wrapping paper, and glue it on to the centre of the card.

8 Tear a 2.5x2.5cm (1x1in) square, and a 2.5x5.5cm (1x2¼in) rectangle of blue handmade paper. Glue them to the front of a sea-green card, in the top right and bottom left corners. Draw a dashed gold metallic line around the blue paper square and rectangle. Glue lengths of dried grass and seed heads on to the blue panels.

9 Cut a piece of coloured corrugated card 7.5x7.5cm (3x3in) and glue it to the centre of a yellow card. Glue three mosaic tiles in the centre of the corrugated card. Glue a button or flat object on to the centre of each tile.

10 Cut a square of ginger silk fabric 4x4cm (1½x1½in) and pull away some of the thread to fray the edges. Glue the fabric on to the centre of a black card. Using a ruler and metallic pen, draw a gold line around the edges of the card front. Glue a small stone or bead in the centre of the silk.

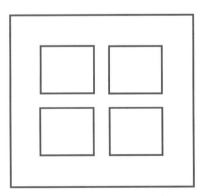

Use these outlines to make window-shaped templates for your cards.

3-D Greetings

Stamping is ideal for producing the multiple images needed for 3-D découpage. Stamp the images with black or coloured ink, or emboss them for a stronger outline. Choose stamps with clear images and plenty of space between the outlines for adding colour, or make your own. (See Techniques pages 20 and 44)

You will need

- Greetings card blank
- Thick paper
- Wooden plant tag – chopstick
- Napkin ring
- Gift box
- Small spice seeds
- Rubber stamps
- Ink stamp pad
- Stamping ink – black
- Embossing stamp pad and embossing ink
- Embossing powder – bronze
- Small scissors, craft knife
- Cutting mat, tweezers, paintbrush
- Acrylic paint – pink, blue
- Varnish – clear matt, glitter glue
- Silicone glue or double-sided fixing tabs
- Felt-tipped pens – yellow, red, blue, green, orange, brown, black, pink
- PVA glue or spray adhesive

Making a stamped image

1 To make a 3-D picture choose stamps that are similar to those used for this project. Spread the ink pad with stamping ink and allow it to soak well into the pad before using.

2 Take your chosen stamp and press on to the ink pad; remove from the pad and stamp it on to thick paper or thin card, before lifting carefully off. You may want to practise applying the stamp until you achieve an even application. You will need approximately six copies of the image.

3 Allow the ink to dry and then colour the image with felt-tipped pens before cutting out the design, following the instructions on page 22. Wash the stamp in warm soapy water to remove the excess ink, and dry completely.

Making an embossed image

1 Spread embossing ink on to a clean stamp pad and allow to soak in thoroughly.

2 Press the stamp on to the pad and then on to thick paper or thin card. Before the ink dries, sprinkle embossing powder over the stamped design, leave for a few seconds then tap off the excess powder, returning it to the pot. Practise the process several times on a spare piece of paper until you manage to achieve a good clean image.

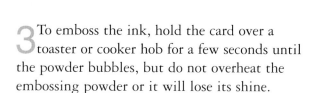

3 To emboss the ink, hold the card over a toaster or cooker hob for a few seconds until the powder bubbles, but do not overheat the embossing powder or it will lose its shine. Allow to dry, then colour the image.

Colouring the stamp

1 Look at the stamped design and decide which areas are in the background, which are in the foreground and which are in between.

2 The upper layers of the picture will need more detailed colouring than the lower layers. It will also be necessary to colour the cut edges of the paper pieces, otherwise they will show as white in the picture (see Finishing Techniques, page 26). With some of the smaller pieces it may be easier to colour the design before cutting it out.

Applying the layers

1 Having planned your design carefully, cut out a base layer, using scissors; for the smaller pieces you may find it easier to use a sharp craft knife and cutting mat. Stick this layer flat on to your chosen surface using PVA glue or spray mount.

2 Colour and cut a second layer in the same way, and fix it exactly over the base layer: use the end of a cocktail stick to apply 5mm (¼in) blobs of silicone to the base layer. Position the paper piece on to the silicone blobs using tweezers; do not press the paper down or the silicone will spread and may show in the picture. Use a cocktail stick to nudge the paper piece into position; try to get the piece exactly over the shape underneath (see Building a Picture, page 24). Continue adding layers in the same way. Apply the silicone to the base layers, not to the back of the paper pieces. Take care to keep the silicone away from the edges of the design.

Making the card

1 Stamp and emboss six copies of a house design. Colour the images as before.

2 Cut out and fix the base layer centrally on to the front of a greetings card using PVA glue or spray adhesive. Add a second layer as before using silicone blobs.

3 For the third layer, cut out the house, removing the house wall, but leaving the windows, roof, door, steps and railings. Fix in place using silicone. For the fourth layer cut as before, then remove the roof, window panes and door: this leaves the window frames, window boxes, door pillars, steps and railings.

4 The fifth layer consists of just the shutters, door pillars, steps and railings, and the final layer is the front step and railings. Decorate the edge of the card with a line of glitter glue.

Making a plant tag

1 Cut a rectangle of card slightly larger than your stamped image or the part of the image that you are using; glue a wooden chopstick to the back using PVA glue. Paint with two coats of pink acrylic paint and one coat of matt varnish, leaving to dry between coats.

2 Stamp or emboss your design six times on to paper or card, then colour with felt-tipped pens.

3 Cut out the base layer carefully and fix on to the plant tag with PVA glue or spray adhesive. Cut more layers, leaving off some parts of the design as you work forward with the layers. In this example, the butterfly is the final layer.

Making the napkin ring

1 Paint a wooden napkin ring with two coats of blue acrylic paint, allow to dry and then apply a coat of clear matt varnish.

2 Choose a small design or part of a design, similar to the sunflowers in the picture, to decorate the napkin ring. Stamp or emboss four copies of the design as before.

3 Colour the design, then cut out and apply the base layer to the napkin ring using PVA glue or spray adhesive, then allow to dry. Apply more layers using silicone glue, cutting

away parts of the design as you move forward with the layers.

4 For a floral design you can add extra interest to the final layer using spice seeds. Paint the seeds black then glue them on to the centre of the flower using PVA glue.

5 As the napkin ring will be subjected to heavy use, for extra protection seal the design with a coat of clear matt varnish or clear nail polish (see Finishing Techniques, page 26).

Decorating the gift box

1 Paint a small gift box with two coats of yellow acrylic paint, and the lid with blue, then finish with a coat of matt varnish, leaving to dry between coats.

2 Choose a design that will fit the box top. Stamp or emboss this design six times, then colour using felt-tipped pens. Cut more layers, removing parts of the design as you move forward with the layers. Fix the layers as before.

Glittering Christmas Cards

The handmade paper used for this project was made from paper pulp that contained paper napkins and tinsel. Stencils wre used to print the star, the Christmas tree and the holly, which were then embossed and highlighted with gold rubbing paste for a co-ordinated and sophisticated look. (See Techniques pages 10, 28 and 52)

You will need

- Envelopes and card – brown
- Paper napkins – red and green
- Paper for making pulp
- Bucket, piece of wood or hand-held liquidizer
- Plastic tray to use as a vat
- Kitchen cloths, rectangles of hardboard
- Clean bricks or heavy weights
- Mould and deckle
- Rolling pin, sponge
- Star-shaped stamp
- White writing paper
- Powder poster paints – red and green
- Tinsel – gold
- Metallic paint – gold
- Thin ribbon – gold
- Rubbing paste – gold
- Blank stencil card
- Light-box or window, embossing tool
- Craft knife, cutting mat, pencil, ruler
- Newspaper, tacky glue, water

Making the paper

1 Prepare the paper pulp as described on page 13. Pour the pulp and water into the vat. Tear red paper napkins into small squares and add them to the pulp; stir well. For a stronger colour, add red powdered poster paint to the pulp, again stirring well to mix in the powder.

2 Remove some of the strands from a length of tinsel, and drop them on to the surface of the pulp just before making each sheet of paper (see Making a Sheet of Paper, pages 14–16). Make the green paper in the same way. For this project you will need five sheets of red paper and five sheets of green paper.

Making the holly card

1 Cut a piece of red handmade paper 18x25cm (7x10in) giving the edges a torn effect. To do this, fold the paper where you want the tear to be, dampen with water and then tear along the fold. Fold the paper exactly in half.

2 Make a tracing of the holly design on page 77. Transfer the design on to stencil card and then cut along the outlines, leaving leaf- and berry-shaped holes cut in the card.

3 Tear a piece of green paper 8.5x13cm (3¹/₄x5in). Hold the stencil firmly on to the middle of the paper. Using a small piece of

sponge, dab gold rubbing paste on to the paper through the holes cut in the stencil. Leave the card to dry.

4 Place the paper, with the stencil still in position, on a light box (or against a window) so that the stencil is face down, and you are working from the reverse side of the design. Draw around the edges of the design, using an embossing tool, pressing as hard as you can without tearing the paper. Depending on the thickness of the paper it may not be possible to see through the paper, in which case 'feel' your way round the edges with the tool. Rub over the rest of the design as though colouring with a pencil, making the leaves and berries slightly concave from the back.

5 Carefully remove the stencil from the green paper. Glue the embossed green paper on to the centre front of the red card. To finish the card, cut a piece of white writing paper slightly smaller than the card; fold it in half and glue it inside the card along the spine.

6 To make the matching envelope, cut a piece of red paper 6x7cm (2½x2¾in), tearing the edges as before. Glue this to the top left–hand corner of the envelope. Tear a piece of green paper 4.5x4.5cm (1¾x1¾in). Make a stencil of

the small holly leaf on the opposite page. Stencil and then emboss the holly leaf on to the paper. Glue it to the centre of the red paper on the envelope.

Making the tree card

1 Cut a piece of red handmade paper 18x25cm (7x10in), tearing the edges as before. Fold the paper in half.

2 Make a stencil of the Christmas tree design opposite. Cut a piece of green handmade paper slightly larger than the tree; stencil and then emboss the tree on to the paper. Cut round the gold embossed tree leaving a margin of about 3mm (⅛in) around the edges. Glue the tree on to the card. Glue a piece of folded white paper inside the card in the same way as for the holly card.

3 To make the matching envelope, tear a piece of red paper 5.5x5.5cm (2¼x2¼in) and glue it at an angle on the top left-hand corner of the envelope. Stencil and then emboss the gold star from the top of the Christmas tree on to a piece of green handmade paper. Cut it out with a margin of 3mm (⅛in) and glue it to the centre of the red diamond.

Making the star card

1 Cut a piece of green handmade paper 18x25cm (7x10in), tearing the edges as before. Fold it in half. Tear a piece of red handmade paper 7.5x13.5cm (3x5½in) and glue it to the front of the green card.

2 Stencil, then emboss the star on to the red handmade paper. Cut out the star leaving a small margin of red paper around the design. Cut out the centre of the star using a craft knife; put this small star to one side. Glue a piece of green paper behind the cut-out smaller star. Glue the star to the centre of the card.

3 Tear a 5x6cm (2x2½in) rectangle of green paper and glue it to the top left corner of the envelope. Tear a red rectangle 3x4cm (1¼x1½in) and glue this to the centre of the green. Glue the small star (cut from the larger one in step 2) on to the envelope.

Making the paper and tags

1 Paint a thin layer of gold paint on to the surface of your star-shaped stamp and press it down firmly on to a piece of handmade paper. Add more paint to the stamp and stamp the paper again. Repeat the process until the paper is covered with stars. Once dry, the paper can be used as gift-wrap.

2 To make the tag, cut a rectangle from stamped paper and the same sized rectangle from card. Glue the two together, punch a hole in one corner and thread with gold ribbon.

Use these Christmas shapes to cut stencils for decorating your handmade paper.

Organic Nature Cards

Handmade paper, dried flowers, twigs and raffia have been used to make these natural-looking cards, envelopes and tags. Decorated with fruit, butterflies and ladybirds cut from handmade paper, they are sure to be a hit with anyone who enjoys nature and the countryside. (See Techniques pages 10 and 28)

You will need

- Handmade paper – dark green, light green, natural, light blue, red, mustard yellow, mauve, terracotta, cream, light brown
- Light card – brown
- Twigs, cinnamon sticks, dried flowers, bark, straw
- Natural raffia – open-weave hessian
- Hole punch
- Craft wire – thin
- Permanent marker pen – black
- Ruler, pencil, craft knife, cutting mat, scissors
- Tacky glue

Making the pineapple card

1 Use a pencil and ruler to draw a rectangle 15x25cm (6x10in) on to terracotta-coloured handmade paper. Fold and dampen the paper along the pencil lines, then tear out the rectangle working against a straight-edge. This will give the edges a natural torn finish (see Handmade Paper Card, page 31).

2 Tear a rectangle of natural-coloured paper 8.5x10.5cm (3½x4in). Glue it on to the centre front of the card.

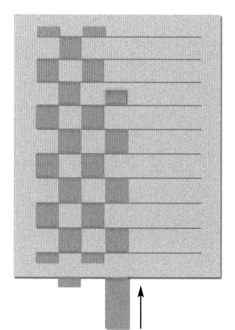

3 The pineapples are made from woven paper; either buy the paper ready made, or make

your own. To do this, cut two pieces of thin handmade paper 15x20cm (6x8in), one in cream and one in light brown. Take the light brown piece and draw a rectangle 1cm ($^3/_8$in) in from the edges using a pencil and ruler. Mark off 6mm ($^1/_4$in) intervals down both short sides of the rectangle. Use these marks to cut parallel slits within the rectangle, joining them on both sides. Now cut strips of cream paper, 6mm ($^1/_4$in) wide and 15cm (6in) long. Weave the lighter strips in between the slits cut in the light brown paper, forming a basket-weave effect.

4 Make tracings of the pineapples on page 82. Cut out the shapes, then lay them on to the basket-weave paper. Draw around the outside edge of the pineapples, and then cut around the edge. Once you have cut out the basket-weave pineapples, you may need to add a small amount of glue to the edges of the paper strips to hold the pineapples together.

5 Make tracings of the pineapple tops. Cut the larger tops from dark green paper and the smaller insides from light green. Cut two narrow strips of dark green paper to go down the centre of the tops. Glue all the pieces on to the front of the card.

6 Cut three lengths of twig or cinnamon stick 6cm (2$^1/_2$in) long and glue these on to the two short sides and top of the card.

Making the envelope

1 Draw a rectangle slightly larger than your card, adding flaps so that when folded over they will make an envelope shape. Cut out the envelope, then score and fold on the dotted lines. Fold the side flaps in and the bottom up and glue the envelope together. (For more details see page 35.)

2 Tear a piece of terracotta-coloured handmade paper 5x6cm (2x2$^1/_2$in) and glue this to the top left-hand corner of the envelope. Tear a slightly smaller piece of natural-coloured paper and glue this to the centre of the terracotta paper. Use the small pineapple trace on page 82 to cut the pineapple from basket-weave paper, and the top from dark and light green paper. Glue the complete pineapple over the rectangle of handmade paper in the corner of the envelope.

Making the gift tag

1 Tear a piece of terracotta-coloured paper 7x9cm (2$^3/_4$x3$^1/_2$in) and make a hole in one corner using a hole punch. Tear a piece of natural-coloured paper 5x6cm (2x2$^1/_2$in) and glue it to the centre of the terracotta paper.

2 Cut a pineapple from basket-weave paper, and the pineapple top from dark and light paper, using the medium-sized pineapple design on page 82. Glue the pineapple in position on the tag, then thread the tag with a length of raffia.

Making the apple card

1 Tear a rectangle 15x25cm (6x10in) of green handmade paper. Score and fold the card in the same way as for the pineapple card. Tear a

rectangle of natural coloured paper 8x12cm (3¼x4¾in) and glue it to the centre front of the card.

2 Cut a piece of thin flat bark or ridged brown paper 8x10cm (3¼x4in) and glue it over the natural-coloured paper. Make a bow from several lengths of raffia and glue it to the top left-hand corner of the bark.

3 Cut the apples and leaves from light green handmade paper. Cut the leaf veins from dark green and the highlights on the apples in white. Glue the apples and leaves on to the front of the card. Cut short lengths of twig or cinnamon stick for the stems, and glue them to the tops and bottoms of the apples.

Making the envelope and tag

1 Make an envelope in the same way as for the pineapple card, adding a rectangle of green and natural paper and a small apple.

2 Tear a rectangle of natural-coloured paper 6x8cm (2½x3¼in). Make the tag in the same way as for the pineapple, adding a rectangle of green paper and a small apple.

Making the ladybird card

1 Tear a rectangle 15x25cm (6x10in) from grey-coloured paper. Score and fold the card in the same way as for the pineapple card. Tear a rectangle of green paper 8x10cm (3¼x4in) and glue it to the centre front of the card.

2 Cut a clover leaf shape from light green paper. Glue this to the card, adding leaf veins in dark green paper. Use the designs on page 83 to cut a large and a medium ladybird from red paper. Glue the ladybirds on to the card, then add spots, head and tail markings, and feet using a black permanent marker pen.

3 Glue two small pieces of twig or cinnamon stick in opposite corners of the card.

Making the envelope and tag

1 Make an envelope in the same way as for the pineapple card, adding a rectangle of green handmade paper, a small green clover leaf and a small ladybird.

2 Tear a rectangle of dark green paper 7x8cm (2¾x3¼in). Make the tag in the same way as for the pineapple tag, adding a small clover leaf and a medium and very small ladybird.

Making the butterfly card

1 Tear a rectangle 15x25cm (6x10in) from mustard-yellow handmade paper. Cut a square of open-weave hessian 9x11cm (3½x4½in) and glue to the centre of the card.

2 Use the design on page 83 to cut a leaf from green paper. Glue a length of thin craft wire on to the back of the leaf for the spine. Make vein marks on the leaf using a blunt tool. Glue the leaf and a spray of dried flowers on to the hessian.

3 Cut a butterfly from mauve paper, the markings from dark blue paper, and a body from cream paper. Use a dark blue pencil to add detail lines to the butterfly wings. Glue the butterfly on to the card, adding two lengths of straw for antennae.

Making the envelope and tag

1 Make an envelope in the same way as for the pineapple card, adding a rectangle of yellow handmade paper and a small butterfly.

2 Tear a rectangle of yellow paper 7x8cm (2¾x3¼in). Make the tag in the same way as for the pineapple, adding a small rectangle of hessian and a small butterfly.

Small Apple

Apples

Use these outlines
to make tracings
for your flora and
fauna cards.

Medium
Pineapple

Pineapples

Small
Pineapple

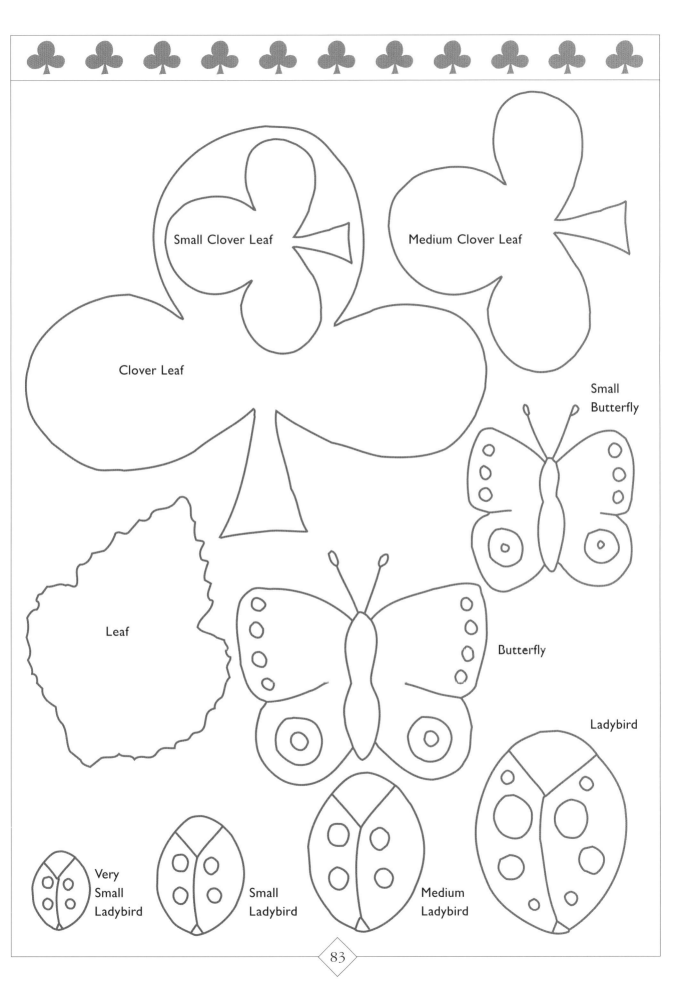

Small Clover Leaf

Medium Clover Leaf

Clover Leaf

Small
Butterfly

Leaf

Butterfly

Ladybird

Very
Small
Ladybird

Small
Ladybird

Medium
Ladybird

Moon and Star Cards

These celestial cards in gold and silver are quick and easy to make in large numbers, yet the final results are stunning. All the cards are simply finished, but the variety of textures, including corrugated card, punched tin and holographic paper, give them added interest. (See Techniques page 28)

You will need

- Triple-fold window cards – 9x12cm (3½x4¾in), 8x11cm (3x4¼in), 11x15cm (4¼x6in)
- Card – silver, dark blue, white
- Paper – dark blue
- Thick card
- Scrap card
- Stationery stars
- Holographic paper – blue
- Holographic card – white
- Curling ribbon – gold, thread – silver
- Marker pen – silver, glitter pen – silver
- Corrugated card, cellophane – blue
- Fuse wire, tin cut from tin food packaging
- Watercolour paper, watercolour paint,
- Container of clean water, paintbrushes
- Sun- and moon-shaped hole punch
- Craft knife, cutting mat, scissors
- Glue gun, tacky glue, pencil, ruler

Making the gold star card

1 Cut a piece of blue holographic paper to fit behind the opening in a 9x12cm (3½x4¾in) window card. Glue it to the back of the window, inside the card. Turn one flap of the card over on to the back of the holographic paper and glue it in place.

2 Cut three lengths of gold curling ribbon approximately 12cm (4¾in), 8cm (3in) and 6cm (2½ in) long. Attach the lengths of ribbon to the card, in the top right-hand corner of the holographic paper, using a gold stationery star.

3 Twist the longest length of ribbon into a spiral and secure the end to the bottom left-hand corner of the card using a gold star. Twist the shortest ribbon and attach it to the bottom right-hand corner with another star. Twist the last length of gold ribbon and attach it in the same way, half way up the left-hand edge.

Making the shooting star card

1 Cut a rectangle 11x15cm (4¼x6in) of silver card, score and fold in half (see Making a Card Mount, page 30).

2 Roughly tear a piece of watercolour paper to fit on to the front of the card. Use dark blue and purple watercolour paint to add a wash of colour to the paper. Leave it to dry. Make a tracing of the star numbered five on

the opposite page. Use a craft knife and cutting mat to cut out the star shape from the paper, making a star-shaped stencil.

3 Lay the star stencil on to the bottom left corner of the painted watercolour paper. Use a silver metallic pen to transfer the star shape to the paper by drawing within the cut-away area of the stencil. Draw three straight trail lines behind the star using the metallic pen and a ruler. Glue the watercolour paper to the front of the card.

Making the corrugated card

1 Cut a rectangle 11x15cm (4¼x6in) of blue card, score and fold in half as before. Draw a border around the edges of the card front using a silver marker pen.

2 Cut a piece of corrugated card 3x3.5cm (1¼x1½in) and colour it using the silver marker pen. Make a tracing of the star that is numbered five on the opposite page. Use the tracing to cut a star from corrugated card. Colour the star using silver marker pen. Cut a square of blue cellophane 2x2cm (¾x¾in). Turn the card to a landscape position and glue the silver rectangle in the top left-hand corner of the card. Glue the blue cellophane square towards the top left-hand corner of the corrugated card; glue the silver star in its centre.

Making the five star card

1 Cut a blue rectangle of card 11x15cm (4¼x6in), score and fold in half as before.

2 Draw a rectangle on to the front of the card using a silver glitter pen and a ruler (see Drawing an Outline, page 34).

3 On white paper make a tracing of the star numbered five. Transfer the star to white card and cut out using a craft knife and cutting

mat. Colour the star using a silver glitter pen. Cut a square of thick card small enough to fit behind the glitter star. Glue the star-shaped card on to the back of the star, and then glue the star in the top left corner of the card.

4 Make stencils of the stars numbered one to four. Use these stencils and a silver marker pen to draw four stars in a straight line, radiating down from the glitter star glued in the top left corner of the card.

Making the hanging star card

1 Cut a piece of dark blue paper to fit behind the opening in a 11x15cm (4¼x6in) double-folded window card (see page 30). Outline the window with a line of silver glitter.

2 Make a tracing of the star numbered six opposite. Use this tracing to cut out two star shapes from silver holographic paper. Apply silver glitter pen around the edges of both stars.

3 Cut two lengths of silver thread 5cm (2in) and 8cm (3in) long. Glue a piece of thread to the back of each star. Now glue the ends of the thread inside the card, so that the star hangs down in the window. Glue the piece of dark blue paper over the window in the card, then fold in the flap and glue it in place.

Add small spots of glitter glue to the blue paper in the card window.

Making the tin star card

1 Cut a rectangle of silver card 11x15cm (4¼x6in), score and fold in half as before.

2 Tear a rectangle of dark blue paper to fit on to the card, and glue it at an angle to the front of the card.

3 Use the tracing of the star numbered six to cut out a star from thin tin sheeting. The tin can be bought from a craft shop, or you can cut it from food packaging. Put the tin star face down on a scrap of thick card, then use a pencil to draw a pattern of dots and lines on the back of the star, making indentations in the tin.

4 Cut a piece of fuse wire 10cm (4in) long. Wind the wire around a knitting needle to make a stretched coil spring. Use a hot glue gun to glue the spring to the back of the star, and then the star to the blue paper on the front of the card.

Making the tin moon card

1 Cut a rectangle of silver card 11x15cm (4¼x6in), score and fold in half as before.

2 Cut a piece of dark blue paper slightly smaller than the front of the card. Glue the paper in the bottom right corner of the card, so that there is a wider border at the top and down the left side of the blue paper.

3 Make tracings of the star numbered five and of the moon, and use these tracings to cut out shapes from tin. Place the tin shapes face down on a scrap of card and use a pencil to make indentations on the star and to draw a face on the moon. Glue the star and moon on the front of the card using a glue gun.

4 Use a sun- and moon-shaped hole punch to make five suns and four moons from dark blue paper. Glue them on to the border edge on the front of the card using tacky glue.

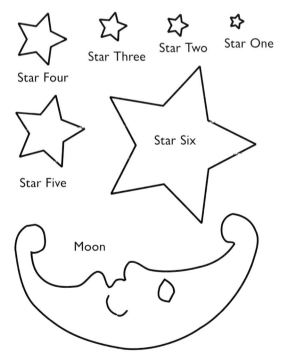

Use these outlines to cut star and moon shapes from paper, card and tin.

Notes from the Garden

These pretty display cards with pots of flowers are just the thing to give a keen gardener. Fill the pots with a selection of small dried flowers, then the card can be framed and hung in the conservatory or garden room as a year-round reminder of summer in the garden. (See Techniques page 28)

You will need

- Card – cream, light green, dark green, light blue, turquoise and terracotta
- Dried flowers
- Self-adhesive sticky pads
- Double-sided sticky tape
- Pencil, ballpoint pen, white paper
- Ruler, white paper
- Scissors
- Craft knife, cutting mat
- Tacky glue

Making the card

1 Cut a rectangle of pale-coloured card 16.5x17cm (6^1/$_2$x6^3/$_4$in). Draw a fine pencil line midway across the width of the card. Score along this line using a straight-edge and the back of a craft knife (see Making a Card Mount, page 30). Fold the card along the score line. Make the larger card in the same way using a 24x17cm (9^1/$_2$x6^3/$_4$in) rectangle of card.

2 Make a tracing of the large or small card design on pages 90 and 91 on to white paper using a ballpoint pen. Place the tracing on to the front of the folded card and draw over the dotted lines, pressing hard enough to make indentations in the card. Draw over the indentations with a pencil. Cut out the marked rectangle in the centre of the card: this will be the window opening. Use the tracing to cut a window frame from coloured card. Glue the frame over the opening on the front of the card.

3 Make a tracing of the large or small canopy on page 91. Transfer the design lines on to card and cut out the canopy. Score along the dotted line at the top and then fold the tab over on to the reverse side. Make a crease along the lower dotted line. Glue the tab to the card using double-sided sticky tape: the top of the canopy should be level with the card top. Attach the bottom edge of the canopy to the card using self-adhesive sticky pads.

4 Make a tracing of the large or small steps on the opposite page. Transfer the design lines to coloured card and cut out the steps. Score along the dotted lines, then fold the top and bottom tabs over on to the back of the steps before concertina-folding along the remaining score lines to make steps.

5 Attach a row of self-adhesive sticky pads across the card, 1.25cm (½in) below the pencil line drawn across the bottom of the card. Use double-sided sticky tape to attach the top and bottom tabs on the back of the steps to the card, so that the top step is level with the pencil line and supported on the sticky pads.

6 Make a tracing of the plant pot and another of the plant pot rim on the opposite page. Use the tracings to cut the pot and the rim from terracotta-coloured card. Glue the rim on to the pot. Make a small slit in the pot just above the rim, which is shown as a dotted line on the diagram.

7 Cut dried flowers into short lengths and insert the stems through the slit at the top of the pot. Glue the stems on to the back of the pot. Make three pots for the smaller card, and five for the larger. Attach them to the steps using self-adhesive sticky pads which will space them away from the card.

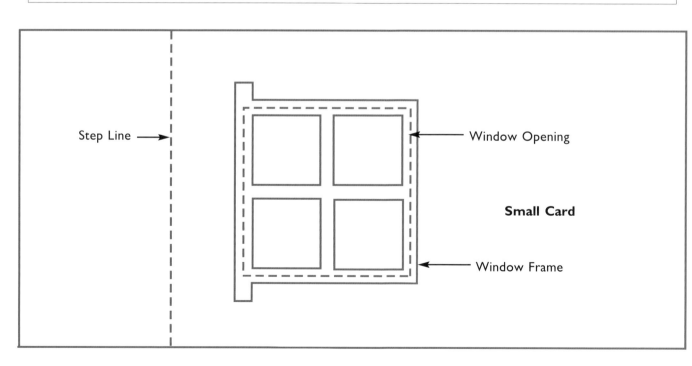

Step Line →

Window Opening

Small Card

Window Frame

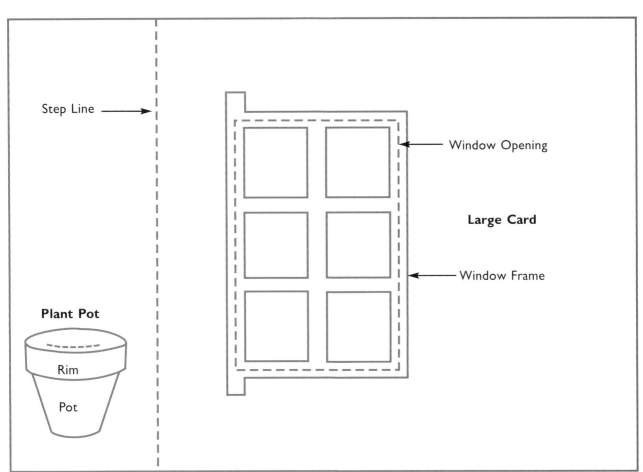

Step Line

Plant Pot

Rim

Pot

Large Card

Window Opening

Window Frame

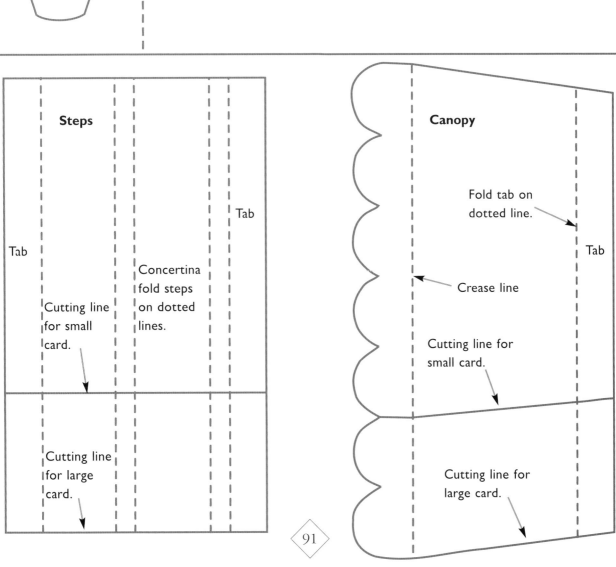

Steps

Tab

Tab

Concertina
fold steps
on dotted
lines.

Cutting line
for small
card.

Cutting line
for large
card.

Canopy

Fold tab on
dotted line.

Tab

Crease line

Cutting line for
small card.

Cutting line for
large card.

GIFT PRESENTATION

E veryone loves to give presents, and the way they are wrapped is often as impressive as the gift inside. To make sure your presents are as memorable for their presentation as for their contents, try creating your own tailor-made gift-wrap, bags and boxes, with cards and tags to match – your gifts will look too good to open!

★ **Lacy Wrapping and Cards** (page 94) use pretty paper doilies to create an effect that can be bold and bright, or subtley shimmering.

★ **Citrus Bags and Paper** (page 98) are stamped with real fruit to produce a mouthwatering pattern ideal for zesty gifts.

★ **Strawberry Gift Holders** (page 102) take the craft of 3-D découpage a step further, using plain and printed fabric instead of paper to create gift containers with a difference.

★ **Vegetable Caskets** (page 106) are a fun way to present gifts. Papier mâché is used to re-create vegetables which can be used to hide all sorts of treasures.

★ **Pansy Gift Tags** (page 110) will delight anyone with a passion for flowers, with their realistic blooms created using 3-D découpage.

★ **Fold 'n' Dye Gift Bags** (page 114) will be a hit with teenagers, who will love the tie-dye effect produced on a variety of bags, boxes and gift-wrap using all sorts of dyes.

★ **Mini Gift Bowls** (page 120) are ideal for making in quantity. These papier mâché bowls would make great gifts for children to take home from parties – they could even be made by the kids themselves!

Lacy Wrapping and Cards

This gift-wrap is ideal for Christmas. To make wrap for other gift-giving occasions, use different colours of paper and spray paint: try primary coloured paint on white paper for fun birthday wrapping or white on silver for a wedding gift. (See Techniques pages 28 and 52)

You will need

- Paper for stencilling – white, cream, gold
- Card for making greetings cards and tags – white, gold
- Luggage tags – white
- Gift box – plain white, cream, gold
- Paper doilies
- Spray mount adhesive
- Lighter fuel and cotton buds – for cleaning off the glue
- Spray paint – copper, gold
- Ribbon – copper, gold
- Cabochon jewellery stones
- White tracing paper, soft pencil
- All-purpose glue, newspaper, scissors

Stencilling with the doily

1 Cover your work surface with plenty of newspaper or scrap paper. When using spray adhesive or spray paint, always work in a well ventilated room.

2 Lightly spray the back of a doily with spray mount adhesive. Position the doily right side up on a sheet of paper. Continue adding doilies to the paper in this way, either overlapping the edges or positioning them close together, until the paper is covered. The adhesive will stop the doily from moving in the breeze from the spray paint.

3 Spray paint should always be stored at room temperature; shake it well before using. Hold the can upright and spray from a distance of 30–46cm (12–18in) from the paper. Spray the doily and the paper between evenly (see Using a Doily, page 57). Leave for a few seconds, then carefully peel off the doilies. Leave to dry.

4 If the spray adhesive has made the stencilled paper sticky, dab it away carefully using lighter fuel on a cotton bud; do not rub the paper or the paint may smudge.

5 Use the stencilled paper to gift-wrap presents and cover gift boxes. If you have a plain card gift box, you may prefer to stencil directly on to the surface of the box.

Tie with sheer bronze or gold ribbon and label with luggage tags that have been stencilled in the same way as the paper, or make your own from white card (see page 97).

Making the jewelled cards

1 Trace over the crown and star shape on page 97 on to white paper with a soft pencil. Carefully cut out the shapes from the paper. Hold the cut shapes on to the doily-stencilled paper and draw around the outside edge with the pencil. Then remove the shapes and cut around the pencil line.

2 Cut a rectangle of gold card 25x17cm (10x6½in) and a rectangle of white card 25x12.5cm (10x5in). Score centrally across the width of the cards and fold in half along the scored lines.

3 Stick the crown centrally to the front of the gold card and the star centrally to the front of the white card. Glue jewellery stones to the points of the crown and the centre of the star.

Making a stencilled tag

1 To make a stencilled tag, trace off the tag shape at the bottom of this page, then draw the shape on to the white card. Cover with part of a doily, then spray with the gold or copper paint. When making tags, it will save time and paper if you trace several on to the paper before spraying. Make a hole in the top of the tag and thread with ribbon.

Making a stencilled gift box

1 Lightly spray the back of a doily with spray mount adhesive, then wrap it around one corner of the gift box. Cut away any doily that is not stuck to the box. Continue adding doilies close together, but not overlapping, until the box is covered. To cover the lid, position a single doily on top, wrapping it down over the sides.

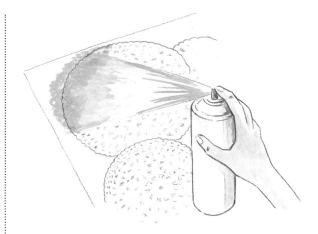

2 Spray with the gold or copper paint. Leave for a few seconds, then carefully peel off the doilies. Leave to dry then decorate with ribbon and a matching tag.

Use these shapes to make cards and gift tags.

Citrus Bags and Paper

There's no need to make a special stamp for this project, as the shapes used on these bags are all produced with real fruit. These handmade bags are quick and easy to stamp and can be made from lining paper, costing you next to nothing. (See Techniques page 44)

You will need

- Sheets of white or cream paper, lining paper
- Fruit – orange, lemon, lime, star fruit
- Acrylic or poster paint – green, yellow, orange
- Cord – for the handles
- Raffia, wool or string – for the tassel
- Card – small piece to make the tassel
- Book – to use as a pattern for the gift bag
- Double-sided tape
- Hole punch
- Chopping board, sharp knife
- Paintbrush or foam roller
- Flat dish for paint
- Container of clean water
- Kitchen paper
- Scrap paper
- Scissors

Preparing the fruit

1 Almost any citrus fruit can be used as a stamp: the fruit should have a firm skin and an interesting internal structure. Vegetables can also be used as stamps: try using peppers, tomatoes or aubergines printed in hot spicy colours.

2 Using a sharp knife and working on a chopping board, cut the fruit in half and lay the pieces cut side down on kitchen paper to absorb the juice.

Stamping with fruit

1 Pour a small quantity of paint into a dish. Load the roller with paint then coat the cut surface of a piece of fruit, making sure the paint is not too thick. Alternatively, use a paintbrush to coat the surface of the fruit, taking care to apply the paint evenly.

2 To achieve the best results, practise stamping on scrap paper before you start the project. Position the fruit on the paper and press down firmly and evenly. Remove carefully to prevent the paint from smudging. You may have to increase or reduce the paint on the stamp depending on the imprint left on the paper. The stamp may need to be loaded with paint between each print, or it may only need loading after a few applications. This will depend on the thickness of the paint, the absorbency of the paper you are using and the natural moisture in the fruit.

3 On white paper or lining paper begin stamping: use different combinations of shapes and colours on each sheet of paper, randomly or in uniform rows to create interesting patterns. Leave to dry.

Making the gift bag

1 You can make just about any size of gift bag, but you will need a book to use as a pattern, over which to create the bag. Choose a book that you can wrap a piece of stamped paper around, overlapping the sides and leaving approximately 2.5cm (1in) along each edge.

2 Spread the paper flat on the table, fold over one long edge, and hold in place with double-sided tape. This will be the top edge of the bag.

3 Wrap the paper around the book, with the folded top edge lined up with the top of the book. Secure the overlapped side edge with double-sided tape. Leave the top folded end open.

4 At the bottom end, fold in each corner of the paper, as you would when wrapping a present. Secure with double-sided tape. Crease the paper bag on each of the edges of the book.

5 Slide the book out of the bag. Flatten the bag and bring the side edges together to create a v-shaped indentation on each side of the bag.

6 Punch handle holes on the top edge of the bag: two on the front side and two corresponding on the back.

7 For the handles, cut two lengths of cord. Thread the cord through the holes in the bag, knotting the thread ends inside the bag.

Making the tassels

1 Wind a length of raffia, wool or string around a short piece of card about 4cm (1½in) wide, twenty or thirty times. You should not be able to see the card through the loops when you stop.

2 Slip a length of raffia, wool or string through the loops at one end of the card. Pull the loops together tightly and make a secure knot to hold them in place.

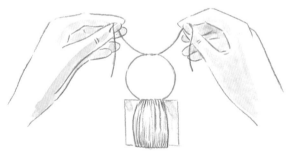

3 Holding the thread tightly on the card, cut through the loops at the bottom end of the card. While still holding the cut ends of the tassel together, carefully remove the card, which can be discarded.

4 Tie a length of raffia, wool or string around the cut loops about 1cm (½in) from the top. Trim across the cut ends to neaten.

5 Slip a long length of raffia, wool or string through the top of the tassel and attach it to a parcel or gift bag.

Stamping the fruit tags

1 Stamp a fruit shape on to paper. Leave to dry. Cut around the outer edge of the fruit.

2 Punch a hole in the top, thread with string or raffia.

3 Alternatively, make a folded tag with the fruit shape stamped on either side. Stamp two fruit shapes close together.

4 When dry, cut around both shapes leaving a small paper bridge between the two. Fold on the paper bridge, bringing the fruit shapes together. Stamp a hole in the top and thread with string or raffia.

5 Fill the present bag with shredded tissue paper, then tie the fruit-stamped tag to the top of the bag.

Strawberry Gift Holders

These pretty 3-D découpage gift holders are a must for summer celebrations; each one is made using a strawberry motif, cut from lightweight furnishing fabric. The fabric is then mounted on to a bag, box or teapot-shaped gift holder. (See Techniques page 20)

You will need

- Lightweight furnishing fabric with a repeat pattern
- Lightweight furnishing fabric 25x20cm (10x8in) – blue
- Medium-weight iron-on interfacing
- Card 25x20cm (10x8in) – blue
- Gift bag – blue
- Gift box – white
- Self-adhesive sticky pads
- White paper, pencil
- White tacky fabric/paper glue
- Glitter glue – red
- Narrow ribbon – red
- Scissors

Choosing the fabric

1 As you will need at least three layers to make the images look three-dimensional, choose a floral fruit fabric with a close pattern repeated. The material should be a lightweight furnishing fabric with a tight weave.

Making the gift bag

1 From the fabric, choose a group of flowers or fruit that will fit the paper gift bag, then cut around the edge, leaving a border of 2cm (1in). Iron medium-weight interfacing on to the back of the fabric, then trim off the surplus with small scissors. This will add stiffness to the design, and prevent the fabric from fraying when cut.

2 Fix the base layer on to the side of the gift bag using white tacky glue; leave to dry.

3 Cut out a second layer exactly the same shape as the first and interface it in the same way. Cut up self-adhesive sticky pads into small pieces, peel off the backing paper on both sides, and stick on to the base fabric. Position the pads close enough together to hold up the fabric without sagging: the closeness of the pads will depend on the thickness of the material you are using.

4 For the third layer, cut out the parts of the design that are furthest forward: on this

fabric these are the two large strawberries at the front of the group, and a smaller strawberry at the top. Fix in place using small pieces of self-adhesive sticky pad.

Making the gift box

1 Choose fabric motifs that will fit on to the sides of the gift box. Iron interfacing on to the back of the fabric, before cutting out the design. The base layer should be stuck in place using white tacky glue; allow to dry.

2 For the second layer cut out the parts of the design that are furthest forward. Attach to the base using self-adhesive sticky pads.

Making the teapot shape

1 Draw over the teapot design opposite and make a tracing on to white paper. Cut out the shape, including the tabs.

2 Cut a piece of blue fabric and interfacing, just larger than the template. Iron the interfacing on to the back of the fabric with a warm iron. Glue thin blue card on to the interfacing on the back of the fabric using white tacky glue; leave to dry. Lay the template of the teapot on to the card side of the blue fabric; draw around the outside and cut out.

3 Fold one tab, along the dotted lines shown on the teapot outline opposite; bend the outer section of the tab inward, and glue it to the inside of the teapot; at the other end of the tab, fold inward on the edge of the teapot, then push the tab in at the centre, making a concertina fold. Repeat for the other tab, then make similar creases on the base, folding along the bottom edge of both teapot halves, making a flat area on to which the teapot can stand.

Cutting the fabric

1 Choose fabric motifs that will fit on to the front of the teapot. Iron interfacing on to the back of the fabric, then cut out several layers of the design. The base layer should be stuck in place using white tacky glue, and the second and third layers positioned using self-adhesive sticky pads. Repeat for the other side of the teapot.

2 Add a line of red glitter glue around the outside edge on both sides of the teapot and along the line of the lid. When the glitter is dry, fill the inside of the teapot with crumpled tissue paper and tie with a ribbon bow.

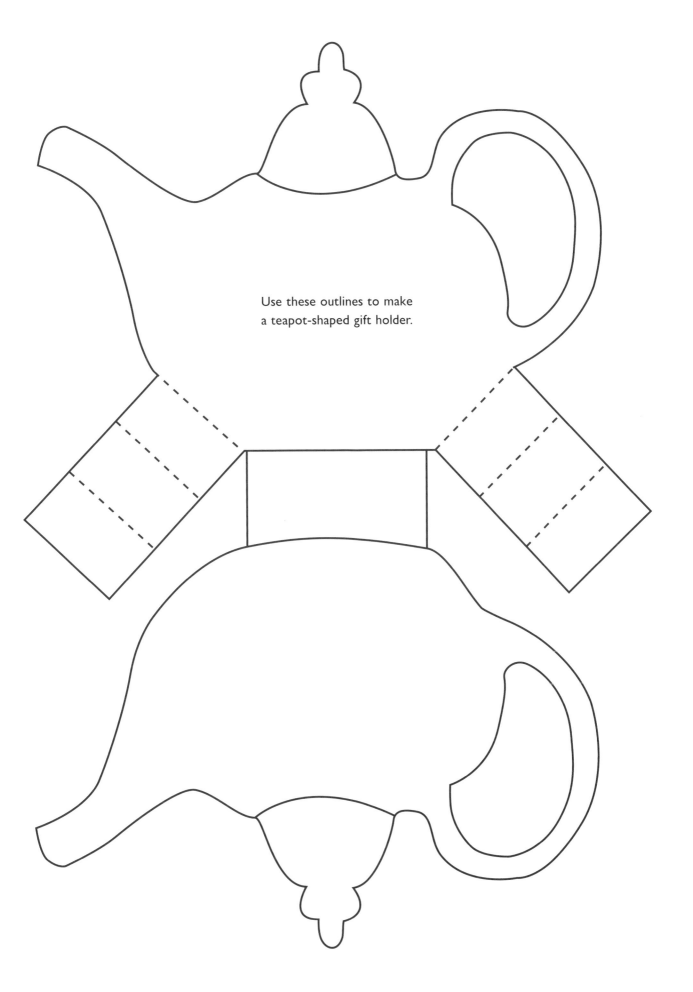

Use these outlines to make
a teapot-shaped gift holder.

Vegetable Caskets

These caskets are made using papier mâché strips over real vegetable moulds. When dry the paper vegetable is cut in half and the real vegetable removed. A brass hinge is then added to make a useful gift box for sweets or chocolates. (See Techniques page 42)

You will need

- Aubergine or pepper
- White emulsion or acrylic gesso
- Acrylic paint – purple, red, green, gold
- Newspaper
- Petroleum jelly
- PVA glue
- Interior wood filler
- Fine sandpaper
- Craft knife
- Water-based gloss varnish
- Two 2cm (¾in) brass hinges
- Thick needle
- Fine brass wire
- Two brass paper fasteners
- Hook fastening

Choosing your vegetable

1 As you will be using a vegetable as a mould for the papier mâché layers, choose one that is a good solid shape, firm and not over-ripe. Almost any fruit or vegetable can be used, but remember when choosing, the more interesting the shape of the vegetable the better the shape of the finished casket will be.

2 Smear your pepper or aubergine liberally with petroleum jelly: this will act as a releasing agent when you remove the vegetable from its mould.

Applying the papier mâché

1 Tear newspaper into strips 6mm (¼in) to 1.5cm (⅝in) wide, and 5cm (2in) long. Mix 3 parts PVA glue to 1 part water and stir until it is the consistency of single cream.

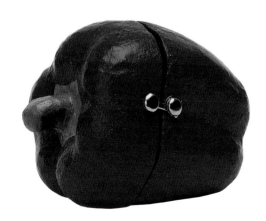

2 Paste the PVA solution on to a newspaper strip and then smooth it on to the vegetable mould. Continue applying the strips of paper, overlapping the edges of all the paper pieces as you work. Apply 10 layers in all, placing each layer in a different direction. Alternating black and white and coloured newspaper strips will enable you to see the different layers more easily. Leave the papier mâché to dry overnight.

3 To make the vegetable look like the real thing, use the wood filler to fill in any irregularities, then when dry, lightly sand the surface to get a smooth finish. Place the paper-covered vegetable on to the table and check that it will stand upright in the correct position: add more filler and sand it smooth until you are happy that it is level.

Removing the vegetable

1 Draw a pencil line around the widest part of the papier mâché vegetable. Using a sharp knife, carefully cut through the papier mâché layer working around the drawn line: do not cut the vegetable, or the juice may leak into the papier mâché. Carefully pull the two halves of the mould apart and gently remove the vegetable (see the diagram on page 108).

Painting the casket

1 Undercoat the casket inside and out with two coats of white emulsion or acrylic gesso, leaving to dry between coats.

2 Paint the insides of both halves of the casket with two coats of gold paint, leaving to dry between coats.

3 Paint the outside of the vegetable casket with two coats of acrylic paint in a colour much brighter than the real vegetable: pillar-box red for the pepper and mauve for the aubergine. On the top edges where the colour meets the gold take care to get a neat line. When dry, paint the stalk area of the vegetable green. Paint the inside and outside of the casket with two coats of gloss varnish.

Making the casket

1 Hold the two sections of the casket together and place the hinge over the join at the back.

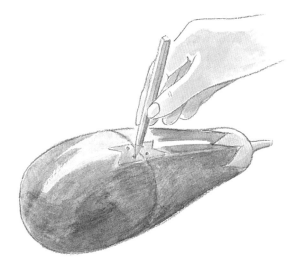

2 Mark the position of the fixing holes on both parts, using a felt-tipped pen. Now, using a thick needle, pierce through the papier mâché layer at these points.

3 Cut two 5cm (2in) lengths of fine brass wire. Take one, bend it in the middle and insert the ends through the lower half of the hinge, then through the holes on one section of the casket. Twist the wire ends together inside the casket. Attach the top half of the hinge to the top section of the casket in the same way.

4 At the front of the casket, make a hole 6mm (¼in) above the join on the top half. Slip the pronged end of the brass paper fastener through the hole in the hook fastening. Insert the prongs through the hole and splay them open on the inside of the casket: although the hook is held firmly, it should have enough slack to turn and engage with the fastener at the bottom.

5 Make a hole at the front of the casket on the lower section and attach a brass paper fastener in the same way as before.

6 Fill the casket with tissue paper and a selection of brightly wrapped chocolates.

Pansy Gift Tags

These delightful, 3-D découpage pansy tags have been hand painted using watercolours. Each has been created from four layers, which are cut from thin watercolour paper. Once painted the pansies are mounted, using silicone, on to parcel labels. (See Techniques page 20)

You will need

- Parcel labels – mixed colours
- Thin watercolour paper – white
- Silicone glue
- White paper, pencil
- Watercolour paints and paintbrush
- Felt-tipped pens
- Scissors, craft knife, cutting mat
- PVA glue or spray adhesive
- Cocktail stick, tweezers

Tracing the pansies

1 Using white paper, trace over the pansy templates on page 113. For each pansy you will have to cut four layers: the base layer is the complete flower; the second layer is minus the petal shape at the back of the pansy; the third layer is the front three petals, losing the back left and right petals; and the final layer is the front petal. Next to the templates on page 113 is a guide showing the four shapes you will need to cut.

2 Once you have traced the four parts of the pansy you are making, cut them out using scissors or a craft knife and cutting mat. This will give four templates for tracing around.

3 Lay the templates on to the watercolour paper and, holding them firmly in position, draw around the outline.

Painting the petals

1 Each layer of the pansy should be painted exactly the same as the one above and below: this is essential as, when assembled, the markings need to flow between layers forming a complete three-dimensional flower.

2 Follow the photograph opposite when you are applying the paint: do not brush the paint across the paper, but let the water in the paint spread it across the image, filling the

shape. If the paint spreads further than the outlines, this can be removed when the petals are cut out. As the centres of the pansies are a different colour to the petals, paint from the centre to the outside, leaving the central area white. When dry paint the centre, leaving a fine line of white paper to form a halo.

3 Add fine vein markings to the petals using felt-tipped pens.

4 When the painted petals are dry, place the paper on a cutting board and cut around the edge of each pansy petal, or group of petals, using a sharp craft knife.

5 Using felt-tipped pens or watercolours, colour the cut edges of the petals so that they are a similar colour to the rest of the flower (see Finishing Techniques, page 26).

Assembling the pansy

1 Attach the base layer of the pansy flat on to a parcel label using PVA glue or spray adhesive. Apply blobs of silicone to the base layer using the end of a cocktail stick. One or two blobs behind each petal should be sufficient – remember to check the shape of the next layer before adding the blobs, as there will be one petal less. Position the second layer on top of the base using tweezers. Do not push down on the petals, but use a cocktail stick to nudge the piece into position so that it lies exactly over the petals beneath.

2 Using silicone blobs, fix the third and then the top layer in the same way.

3 Paint a stem and leaves on to each pansy tag, using dark green watercolour paint.

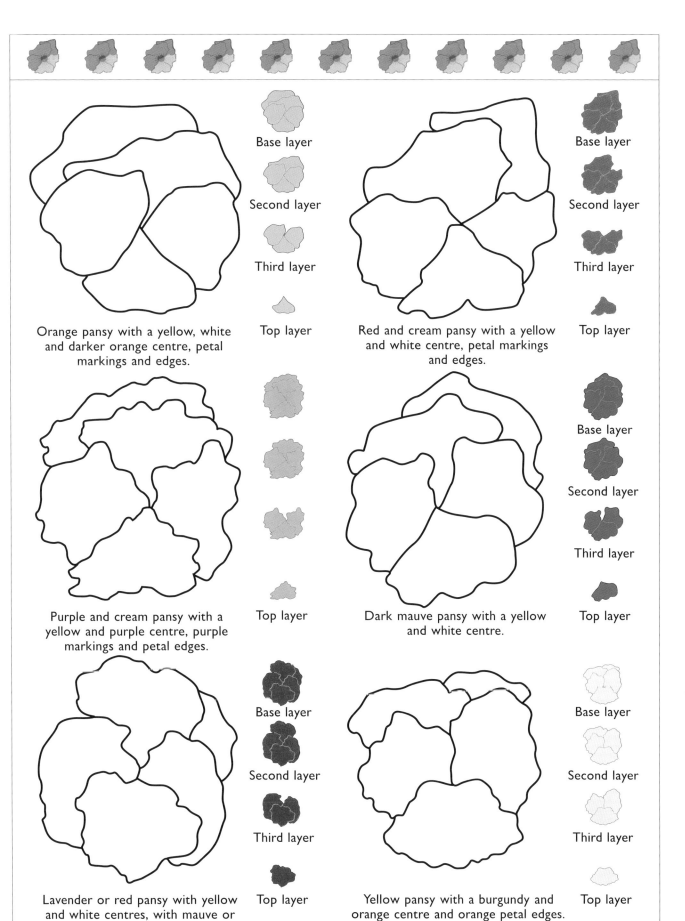

Orange pansy with a yellow, white and darker orange centre, petal markings and edges.

Base layer

Second layer

Third layer

Top layer

Red and cream pansy with a yellow and white centre, petal markings and edges.

Base layer

Second layer

Third layer

Top layer

Purple and cream pansy with a yellow and purple centre, purple markings and petal edges.

Top layer

Dark mauve pansy with a yellow and white centre.

Base layer

Second layer

Third layer

Top layer

Lavender or red pansy with yellow and white centres, with mauve or burgundy markings.

Base layer

Second layer

Third layer

Top layer

Yellow pansy with a burgundy and orange centre and orange petal edges.

Base layer

Second layer

Third layer

Top layer

Fold 'n' Dye Gift Bags

Japanese paper is very absorbent and strong when wet. This makes it ideal for this project where gift bags and boxes are made by folding and dying paper. Food colouring, ink and silk paint can be used on Japanese paper, giving some amazing and very colourful results. (See Techniques page 18)

For this project you will need to dye the following A4 sized sheets of Japanese paper: one for the pyramid box, one for the small bag, and two for the square box. For each larger bag, you will need to dye two A3 sheets.

You will need
- Japanese paper (or paper that is absorbent and strong when wet)
- Thin card or good quality paper
- Raffia ribbon – red
- Dye – food colouring, ink or silk paint
- Hole punch, pencil, ruler
- Rubber gloves
- Newspapers, white paper
- Printing roller or rolling pin
- Small containers for dye
- Clothes peg, elastic band
- Tacky glue
- Iron

Dying the paper

1 Concertina-fold a sheet of Japanese paper from one of the short sides, so that you have a 2cm (³/₄in) wide strip of folded paper. Then concertina-fold the other way until you have a block of folded paper. Hold it together with an elastic band.

2 Protect your work surfaces by covering them with newspaper, and put on a pair of rubber gloves.

3 Food colouring, ink and silk paint can all be used to dye the Japanese paper. Put about 10ml of each of the colours that you will be using into small containers.

4 Remove the elastic band from the concertina-folded paper and, holding the paper tightly between your finger and thumb, dip the corners and edges into each of the coloured dyes: the dye will spread across the paper creating patterns.

5 Place the dyed paper on to newspaper and partially unfold it. Cover the damp paper with a sheet of clean white paper and apply a little pressure with your hand, a roller or rolling pin – this will remove the excess dye and stop it from spreading further across the paper. Now completely unfold the paper and lay it on the newspaper to dry.

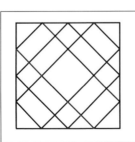

rectangle, then unfold. Fold the opposite sides of the square into the middle and then unfold.

6 Completely unfold the square of paper: the paper will have a grid of folded lines that match the diagram on page 119. Cut along the lines coloured red.

7 Fold in the corners again, and then fold the edges upwards to form the box sides. Lift up each triangle from the centre of the box, tuck under the pointed corner ends and then flap down the triangles. The lid will now stay together, although you can add a dab of glue under the point of each triangle.

Making the pyramid box

1 Glue thin card or paper on to the back of dyed paper.

2 Draw the plan for the pyramid box on page 118 on to the reverse side of the dyed and backed paper. Cut out the design and score along the dotted lines. Using a hole punch, make a hole in the top corner of each triangle.

3 Cut a length of red ribbon approximately 40cm (15in) and thread it through the holes at the top of each triangular side. Pull up the ribbon, bringing the sides of the pyramid together. Tie the ribbon in a bow.

Making the box lid

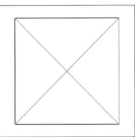

1 Cut a square of paper and draw diagonal lines from corner to corner.

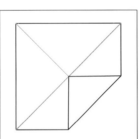

2 Fold in one of the corners of the square to touch the centre point.

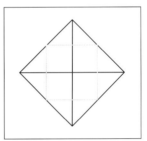

3 Fold in the other three corners to touch the centre point.

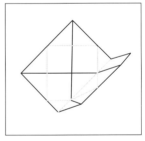

4 Fold the top and bottom edges in, to form a long rectangle, then unfold.

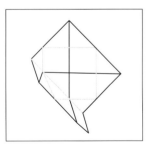

5 Fold in the opposite sides of the square, then unfold.

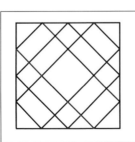

6 Completely unfold the paper: it will now be covered in a grid of lines.

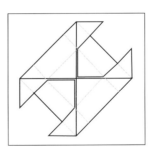

7 Cut along the red lines. Fold the four sides upwards to form the box sides.

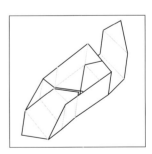

8 Lift up the triangles at the centre point and tuck under the pointed corners.

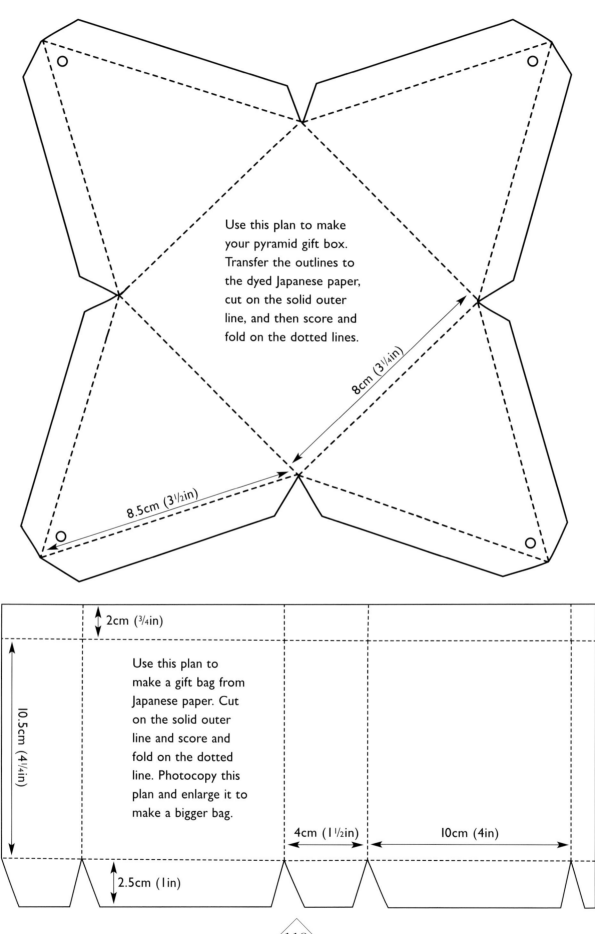

Use this plan to make your pyramid gift box. Transfer the outlines to the dyed Japanese paper, cut on the solid outer line, and then score and fold on the dotted lines.

8cm (3¼in)

8.5cm (3½in)

2cm (¾in)

Use this plan to make a gift bag from Japanese paper. Cut on the solid outer line and score and fold on the dotted line. Photocopy this plan and enlarge it to make a bigger bag.

10.5cm (4¼in)

4cm (1½in)

10cm (4in)

2.5cm (1in)

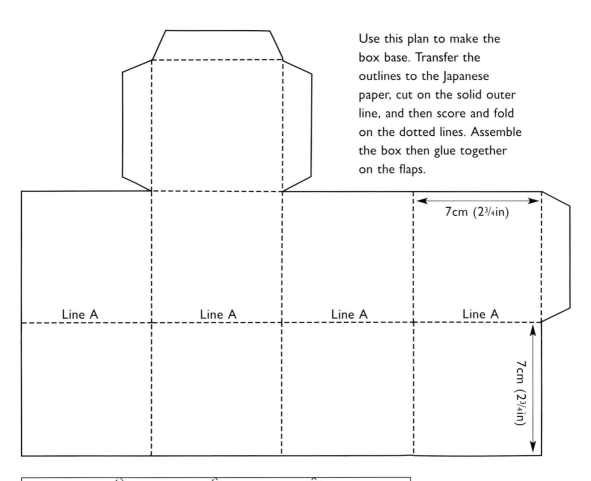

Use this plan to make the box base. Transfer the outlines to the Japanese paper, cut on the solid outer line, and then score and fold on the dotted lines. Assemble the box then glue together on the flaps.

7cm (2¾in)

7cm (2¾in)

Line A   Line A   Line A   Line A

This is the folding and cutting plan for the box lid. Cut on the outer solid line, fold on the dotted lines and then cut on the red lines. See the diagrams on page 117 for detailed folding instructions.

21cm (8¼in) square

Mini Gift Bowls

These fun gift bowls are simple to make from either white or coloured papier mâché pulp, which can be dyed or painted. Once dry, the bowls can be filled with goodies, wrapped in cellophane, then decorated with ribbon. (See Techniques page 36)

You will need

- Ready-mixed papier mâché pulp or white cartridge paper and PVA glue
- Cartridge paper – blue, yellow
- Cold water fabric dye – green, pink, light blue
- Acrylic paint – pink, yellow
- Paintbrush
- Hot water
- Bowl for moulding – china or plastic
- Bowl for mixing pulp
- Petroleum jelly, tablespoon, double-sided tape
- Cloth, clingfilm, rubber gloves
- Small container for mixing dye
- Acrylic varnish – matt

Preparing the moulds

1 Apply a thin coating of petroleum jelly over the surface of a china or plastic bowl. Then wrap the bowl in clingfilm: the jelly will hold the clingfilm in place while you are applying the papier mâché.

Making the papier mâché

1 To make the bowls you can use ready-mixed paper pulp which you can colour with dye. Alternatively, you can make your own pulp from white paper, which can then be dyed or you can make the pulp from coloured paper (see Making Paper Pulp, page 39).

2 To make your own pulp, tear up strips of white, yellow or blue cartridge paper and soak overnight in a bowl of water. Add plenty of water to the mix then use a blender or liquidizer to break it down into a pulp (see Making Paper Pulp, page 38).

3 Strain the pulp to remove excess water, then mix with a small quantity of PVA glue.

Making dyed paper pulp

1 Make up a batch of white paper pulp following the instructions for making pulp above. Wearing rubber gloves, sprinkle an amount of cold water fabric dye into a container, add a teaspoon of hot water and mix with a spoon.

for guidance. Do not apply the pulp too thickly, or the finished bowl will be heavy and chunky.

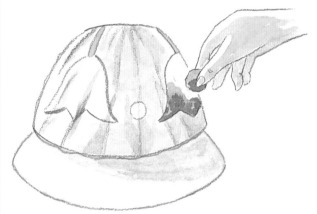

2 Pour a small amount of the dye onto the papier mâché pulp and mix thoroughly. Do not add too much liquid to the pulp or it will become sticky and unworkable. When dry the pulp will be a much lighter shade. When you have made the different coloured pulps, wrap them individually in clingfilm: the pulp will keep for several days if stored in the refrigerator.

Making the tulip bowl

1 Make a large quantity of papier mâché in light blue, pink and green, using dyed or coloured paper.

2 Using the template opposite, cut enough tulip shapes from white paper to fit around the bowl you will be using as a mould. Secure the tulips evenly around the outside of the bowl using double-sided tape. Lightly coat the outer surface of the bowl with petroleum jelly, then wrap in clingfilm. Place the prepared bowl upside down on a larger upturned dish.

3 Make the tulip stems with green pulp and the tulip heads with pink. To apply the pulp, pick up a small amount in your hand and squeeze out the excess water, then press it firmly on to the side of the bowl, using the template

4 Fill in the background in light blue: cover the base first, then work up the sides smoothing the colours together where they meet. Continue adding the pulp until the sides of the bowl are covered. Allow to dry for three days, then carefully remove the mould and peel away the clingfilm. It will be several more days before the bowl is completely dry.

Making the blue star bowl

1 Make a considerable quantity of papier mâché pulp in yellow and blue, using dyed or coloured paper.

2 Trace the star shape opposite on to white paper and cut out the template. For this project the papier mâché bowl is built inside the mould, so you will need to use a clear bowl. Using double-sided tape, fix the template to the bottom of the bowl, with the star points coming up the sides.

3 Lightly coat the inside of the bowl with petroleum jelly, then line with clingfilm.

4 Apply pieces of yellow pulp over the star template in the bottom of the bowl. Work up the points until the star shape is covered.

5 Fill the background of the bowl with blue papier mâché, blending it where the blue and yellow meet. When the pulp is two thirds of the way up the sides of the bowl, add yellow spots, made from 1.5cm (½in) balls of pulp. Press each ball on to the side of the bowl and then flatten. Add blue pulp around the yellow spots, blending the edges together with your finger as you work. Complete the bowl, then allow to dry for three days. Carefully remove the mould and peel away the clingfilm. Leave until completely dry.

Making the yellow star bowl

1 Line the inside of your mould with cling-film as you did for the blue star bowl.

2 Make a quantity of white paper pulp, then press the pulp thinly over the inside surface of the mould.

3 Leave to dry for several days, then remove from the mould. Remove the clingfilm and leave until completely dry.

4 Place the star template on the bottom of the bowl and lightly draw around it with a pencil. Paint the star with yellow, and the bowl with pink acrylic paint.

Sealing the bowls

1 When the papier mâché bowls are dry, seal the surface with matt acrylic varnish.

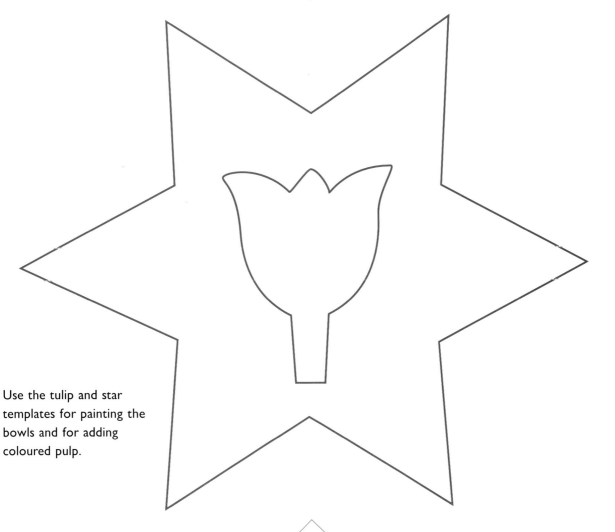

Use the tulip and star templates for painting the bowls and for adding coloured pulp.

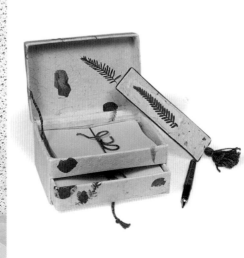

STATIONERY

The shops are full of beautiful stationery and desk sets in a wide variety of styles and colours. However, they tend to be expensive and may not be quite the shape or size required. Making your own, either for yourself or as a gift for someone else, will give you the chance to customize and co-ordinate all your accessories.

★ **Black Cat Accessories** (page 126) uses simple coloured handmade paper, textured with wool. This striking desk set includes a practical folder, pencil pot, note pad and notelet holder.

★ **Batik-Covered Books** (page 132) involve the distinctive and traditional technique of embellishing with batik. Instructions are given for making a portfolio and covering a book.

★ **St Basil's Pen Tidy** (page 136) is made using papier mâché to create the curved domes and spires which are the lids of these handy and attractive storage pots.

★ **Circus Fun Desk Set** (page 142) makes the most of 3-D découpage and tactile crinkle card to bring the circus to life, producing a bright and colourful addition to any child's bedroom.

★ **Petal and Leaf Writing Set** (page 148) is stylish and beautiful stationery made using a range of handmade papers which have both texture and a floral fragrance.

★ **Scrap Paper Photo Albums** (page 152) incorporate a huge variety of scrap materials, mixed into paper pulp, to produce albums with unique and interesting covers.

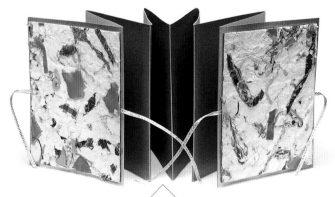

Black Cat Accessories

These desk accessories have been covered with handmade paper, and decorated with geometric borders and black cats. Food colouring is used to colour the paper, and small pieces of cream and white knitting and embroidery wool have been added to give the paper texture. (See Techniques page 10)

You will need

- File
- Note pad or pad of paper and pencil
- Stiff cardboard
- Empty cylindrical container
- 40cm (16in) black ribbon
- Paper for making pulp
- Food colouring – lavender, black
- Knitting and embroidery wool – cream, white
- Mould and deckle, plastic tray to use as a vat
- Bucket, length of wood or hand-held liquidizer
- Kitchen cloths, rectangles of hardboard
- Clean bricks or heavy weights
- Masking tape, scissors, ruler, white paper
- Newspaper
- Ballpoint pen, pencil
- Craft knife and cutting mat
- Tacky glue, water, rolling pin
- Small saw

Making coloured paper

1 Prepare the paper pulp (see Making a Sheet of Paper, page 13). Pour the pulp and the water in to the vat and add a few drops of lavender food colouring, stirring well so as to disperse the colour thoroughly (see Making Decorative Paper, page 17).

2 Cut short lengths of cream and white knitting or embroidery wool and unravel some of the fibres. Give the pulp another good stir and then sprinkle the wool lengths onto the surface of the pulp.

3 Make twelve sheets of lavender-coloured paper (see Making a Sheet of Paper, pages 14–16).

4 As you make the sheets of paper you will need to keep the vat topped up with water, pulp and colouring. You should try to keep the ratio of pulp to water the same as when you started. Stir the pulp between each sheet, adding more strands of wool to the surface.

5 Make two stacks of six sheets, separating each with a damp kitchen cloth. Cover each stack with a piece of hardboard, and weigh down with bricks or heavy books to press out some of the water.

6 Cover your working surface with a sheet of plastic and then a layer of newspaper.

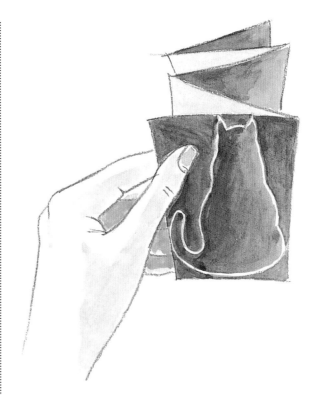

Remove each kitchen cloth with its sheet of paper from the stack and lay them on the protected surface. Leave until almost dry.

7 To give the paper an even surface, roll each sheet with a rolling pin while it is still damp. To keep the paper flat, dry each sheet separately under a weighted board.

8 Make four sheets of black paper in the same way, using black food colouring.

Covering the pencil pot

1 Measure the circumference and height of the container that you will be using for the pencil pot – use a cardboard cylinder container or clean food container. Then cut a rectangle of lavender paper to fit around the outside, which is slightly taller than the container.

2 Apply glue evenly over the outside surface of the container. Wrap the paper around the container, lining it up with the bottom. Smooth out any air bubbles. Apply glue around the inside edge of the container and fold the paper in on to the glue.

3 To cover the inside of the cylinder, you must measure the height and circumference inside the container and cut the paper to fit. Next, apply glue over the surface of the paper, and press the paper in position.

4 Cut a strip of black paper 2cm (³/₄in) wide and long enough to fit around the bottom of the container. Glue the strip in place.

5 Cut squares of lavender paper 1.2x1.2cm (¹/₂x¹/₂in). Cut out a small square from the centre of each one using a sharp craft knife and cutting mat. Glue the large and small squares alternately, on to the black band around the bottom of the container.

6 Make a tracing of the small cat design on page 131 on to white paper. Cut a strip of black paper 4cm (1¹/₂in), and long enough to go round the container. Place the tracing on to the left-hand end of the black paper strip and draw over the design lines with a ballpoint pen, making indentations in the black paper. Concertina-fold the paper to the width of the cat, keeping the cat outline on the top. Make sure the folds are exactly aligned to the edges of the cat. Cut out the cat shape leaving two points uncut as shown on the diagram on page 131. Open out the string of cats, and glue them above the border around the container.

Covering the note pad

1 If your note pad has a hard outer surface, cover it with the lavender paper (see step 3). Otherwise, make a hard cover for the paper pad by cutting two pieces of thick card slightly wider and 6mm (¹/₄in) longer than the pad. For the spine, cut a piece of card the same width as the front and back, and the thickness of the pad.

2 Remove the paper pad from the cover. Line up the three pieces of card with the spine in the centre, leaving a small gap between each to allow for them to fold. Join the pieces together by laying strips of masking tape between the spine and the cover pieces, holding them together. Repeat on the reverse side of the cover.

3 Cut one piece of lavender paper slightly larger than the complete cover. Glue the paper in place, folding the edges over and gluing them on to the inside of the cover. Make a scored indentation in the paper along both fold lines on either side of the spine.

4 Cut a piece of lavender paper for the inside of the cover. Glue this in place and then make scored indentations along the folds.

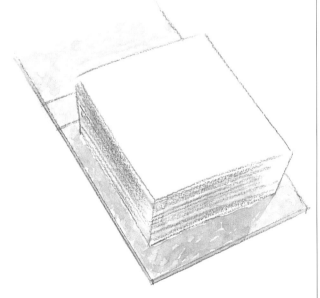

5 Spread glue over the back surface of the paper pad and stick it inside the hard cover.

6 Using a sharp craft knife or small saw, cut a pencil to the same width as the note pad. Cover the pencil with lavender paper. Cut a strip of lavender paper 6x2cm (2$\frac{1}{2}$x$\frac{3}{4}$in) and glue the two ends together, making a loop big enough to hold the pencil. With the pencil in the loop, glue the ends of the loop to the inside back cover, below the paper pad.

7 Cut a strip of black paper 2cm ($\frac{3}{4}$in) wide and the width of the cover. Glue this to the bottom edge of the front cover. Decorate with lavender squares in the same way as for the pencil pot. Transfer the cat design opposite on to the black paper and glue it to the front cover of the note pad.

Covering the file

1 Cover the file with lavender-coloured paper, allowing extra around the edges to turn over on to the inside – depending on the size of the paper and the file, you may need to overlap the paper. Cut lavender paper to fit the inside covers of the file, and glue in place. Make a scored indentation either side of the spine so that the file will fold.

2 Cut two strips of black paper 2cm ($\frac{3}{4}$in) wide and the height of the file, allowing a little extra to turn in at the top and bottom. Glue the strips to the front and back cover on either side of the spine. Cut lavender squares as before and glue them to the black strips.

3 Cut the two cats and the paw-print design opposite from black paper and glue them on to the front cover.

4 Cut a length of black paper 4cm (1$\frac{1}{2}$in) wide and the length of the spine. Make a tracing of the small single cat on to black paper, and concertina-fold it in the same way as for the pencil pot. Cut out the cat, leaving the

two joining points. Unfold the cats and glue them along the spine.

Making the notelet case

1 Using the diagram on the opposite page as a guide, cut two rectangles from stiff cardboard. Score and fold along the scored lines, and then glue the flaps on the larger rectangle onto the smaller one, notched edge towards the outer flap. Use masking tape to strengthen the joins on the inside of the case.

2 Next, cover the outside of the case with lavender-coloured paper.

3 Then cut a 16cm (6$\frac{1}{2}$in) length of black ribbon, and glue one end to the inside middle of the outer flap, against the outer edge. Glue lavender paper over the inside of the flap, covering the glued ribbon end.

4 Cut a 16cm (6$\frac{1}{2}$in) length of black ribbon. Using a sharp craft knife, make a small hole in the back of the folder, 1.5cm ($\frac{5}{8}$in) from the outer edge and lining up with the ribbon at the front. Push one ribbon end through the cut, and glue it inside the case. The ribbon ends can be tied together to hold the case closed.

5 Cut a strip of black paper that is 2cm ($\frac{3}{4}$in) wide and as long as the height of the case. Glue this against the spine on the front cover of the case. Then cut lavender paper squares as you did before, and glue them alternately along the black paper strip.

6 Make a tracing of the cat and butterfly design opposite. Cut them from black paper and glue on to the front of the case.

7 Fill the case with folded note paper and envelopes, or notelets.

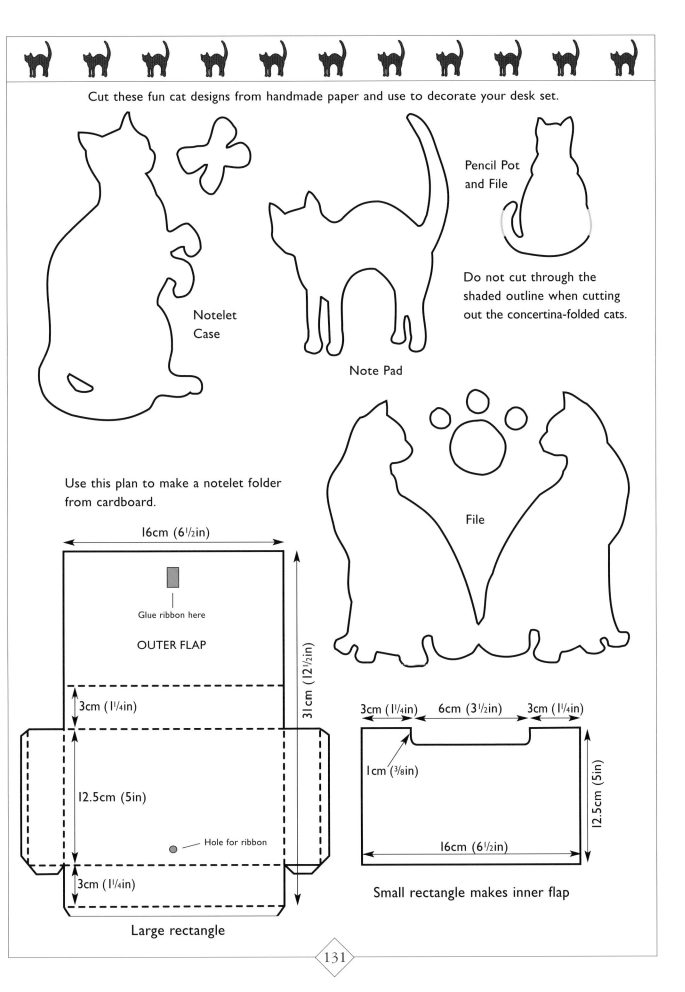

Cut these fun cat designs from handmade paper and use to decorate your desk set.

Notelet Case

Pencil Pot and File

Do not cut through the shaded outline when cutting out the concertina-folded cats.

Note Pad

File

Use this plan to make a notelet folder from cardboard.

16cm (6½in)

Glue ribbon here

OUTER FLAP

31cm (12½in)

3cm (1¼in)

12.5cm (5in)

Hole for ribbon

3cm (1¼in)

Large rectangle

3cm (1¼in)   6cm (3½in)   3cm (1¼in)

1cm (³/₈in)

12.5cm (5in)

16cm (6½in)

Small rectangle makes inner flap

Batik-Covered Books

Batik is a fun way to decorate plain paper. Patterns are created using melted wax, dropped or brushed on to the paper. The paper is then painted and the wax is removed, leaving the areas beneath it the original paper colour. The process can be repeated several times over, creating some amazing colour schemes and patterns

The instructions for covering the portfolio and book are reversible: thus the portfolio cover with the triangular corners can be used to cover the book, and the portfolio can be covered with a single sheet of batik paper.

You will need
- Paper – good quality coloured paper or white paper coloured with a colour wash
- Batik wax
- Double boiler or saucepan
- Clean empty food tins
- Poster paints
- Book, bookcloth, stiff card
- Ribbon
- Saucers
- Paintbrushes
- Newspaper
- Iron, tacky glue, water
- Ruler, scissors, craft knife, cutting mat

Preparing the paper
1 If you decide to use plain white paper, paint it with watery poster paint and allow time for the paper to dry.

Preparing the wax
1 Fill the bottom of a double boiler with water and put batik wax in the top. Alternatively, put the wax in a clean food tin and place the tin in a saucepan of water. Melt the wax on a low heat – never leave the wax unattended, and be careful not to let the water boil dry.

Designing with wax
1 Cover your work surface with newspaper. Squash together the sides of a clean food tin to form a spout. Pour some of the melted wax into the tin, then use it to make patterns on the paper. A criss-cross pattern can be made by pouring wax from the tin in parallel lines across the paper, first in one direction and then in the other. You can also pour the wax in spirals, or let it dribble to form random patterns; make splats by letting the wax fall on to the paper from about 30cm (12in), or use jerking movements to 'throw' the wax out of the tin on to the paper. You may prefer a more controlled application by using a paintbrush dipped in melted wax to make streaks and drips across the paper.

As the wax touches the paper it will dry almost immediately. You may need to reheat the wax from time to time to keep it in liquid form.

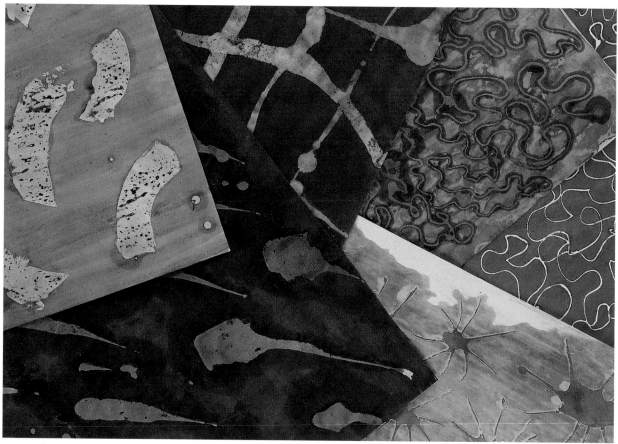

Colouring the paper

1 Choose a paint colour that complements the base colour of your paper. Thin the paint with water and then paint over the batiked paper using long brush strokes. The paint will not stick to the wax pattern; if it does, then you should thin the paint with a little more water. Leave the paper to dry.

Making multicoloured paper

1 Once the wax pattern has been painted over and the paper has completely dried, you can apply another pattern over the top of the first using more wax. Thin a different paint colour with water and then, when the wax has set, paint the paper again. You can repeat this process several times, remembering to dry the paper between each layer of paint and wax.

2 Once the paper is dry, sandwich it between several layers of old newspaper. Put the iron on to a cotton setting and carefully iron the paper – the heat from the iron will melt the wax, which will then be absorbed into the newspaper. This is a very messy process so be careful to protect protect your ironing board and clothing from the melted wax. Keep ironing and changing the sheets of newspaper until all the wax has melted.

Making a portfolio

1 Cut two pieces of thick card 22.5x32cm (8³/₄x12¹/₂in) for the portfolio covers and one piece 2x32cm (³/₄x12¹/₂in) for the spine. Cut a piece of bookcloth 8x35cm (3¹/₈x13³/₄in) making sure that the warp runs parallel to the spine.

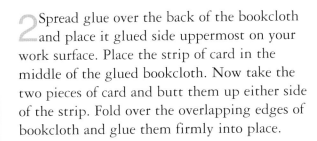

2 Spread glue over the back of the bookcloth and place it glued side uppermost on your work surface. Place the strip of card in the middle of the glued bookcloth. Now take the two pieces of card and butt them up either side of the strip. Fold over the overlapping edges of bookcloth and glue them firmly into place.

3 Cut another piece of bookcloth 8x32cm (3¹⁄₈x12¹⁄₂in) and glue this on to the inside of the spine. Using the corner of a ruler, rub the edges of the bookcloth, making sure it is well stuck down on to the card. Leave the glue to dry.

4 Working on the outside of the portfolio, draw a pencil line 1cm (³⁄₈in) in from each long edge of the bookcloth. Cut a piece of batik paper 22x35cm (8¹⁄₈x13¹⁄₄in) for the front cover; lay the paper on to the cover, lining the long edge up with the pencil line. Cut away a triangle of batik paper at the top and bottom corner of the book, and trim the overlap on the three outer edges to 3mm (¹⁄₈in). Repeat for the back cover.

5 Glue a triangle of bookcloth on to the four corners of the portfolio, slightly larger than the cut away triangles on the batik paper, and with enough overlap to fold over on to the inside. Then glue the paper in position on the covers. Fold the excess paper at the edges over on to the inside, and glue in place.

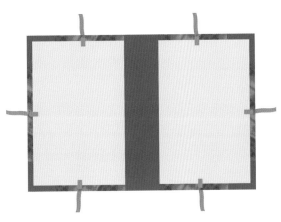

6 To add the ribbons to the portfolio, you will need to make slots to hold them. Cut six slots in all – three for each cover. They should be placed in the middle of each side and 1cm (³⁄₈in) in from the edge. The slots should go through the paper and the card cover. Cut six pieces of ribbon 25cm (10in) long. Thread one through each slot and glue the end of each ribbon on to the inside of the cover.

7 To finish the portfolio, glue a piece of plain-coloured paper 20x31cm (7³⁄₄x12¹⁄₄in) centrally on to the inside of each cover. Place your finished portfolio under a heavy weight, and leave it to dry for at least 24 hours.

Covering a book

1 If possible, try to cover the book in a single sheet of paper. Measure the front and back cover and the spine, adding 3cm (1¹⁄₄in) to the width and 3cm (1¹⁄₄in) to the length. Cut a rectangle of batik paper to this size.

2 Open out the book and then glue the batik paper over the spine and the covers, pressing the paper well down to remove any air bubbles. Fold the excess paper at the edges over on to the inside of the book and glue in place.

3 Finish the book in the same way as the portfolio, leaving it to dry for 24 hours.

St Basil's Pen Tidy

Inspired by the stunning and distinctive rooftops of Moscow, this novel tidy will bring the classic shapes of St Basil's cathedral to your desk top. Beneath the shapely papier mâché towers are cardboard tubes, providing ideal storage for pens, pencils and paper clips. (See Techniques page 36)

You will need a selection of cardboard tubes in various widths and lengths for this project: packing tubes, the inside of toilet rolls, toilet tissue, clingfilm or aluminium foil.

You will need

- Ready-mixed papier mâché pulp or white cartridge paper and PVA glue
- 2mm mounting board
- Cardboard tubes (see above)
- Thin cardboard
- Gloss acrylic paint – brick red, blue, red, green, yellow, white
- Primer – white undercoat
- Metallic paint – gold
- Aluminium baking foil
- Heavy-duty craft knife, cutting mat
- Bradawl, pencils, ruler
- PVA glue
- Fine sandpaper
- Wood screws

Cutting the tubes

Following the plan at the end of the project, cut five buildings from cardboard tubes and five circular lid sections. You can use a ruler and pencil to mark the cutting line around each tube. To ensure your cut is level, attach a pencil

horizontally to the top of a box or other similar object of the right height, then turn the tube holding it against the pencil: this will give a level line around the tube. Sand the cut edges until each section will stand flat on the table.

Assembling the lids

1 Lay the five lid sections on to 2mm mounting board and draw around each one. The diameter of the tubes can be different, as long as you remember that all the pieces of each building and lid must be the same

diameter. Cut out the five discs, slightly larger than the pencil lines, then glue them to the ends of the lid sections.

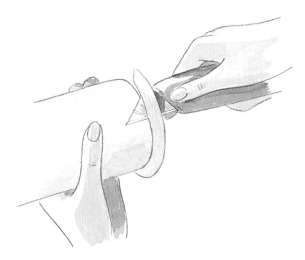

2 After the glue has dried, carefully trim off the excess card using a sharp knife. Use a bradawl to make a hole in the centre of each disc.

Making the conical tower

1 Cut a pencil to a length of 10cm (4in). Sharpen both ends, then glue one end into the hole in the top of the lid section. Leave the glue to dry (see diagram below).

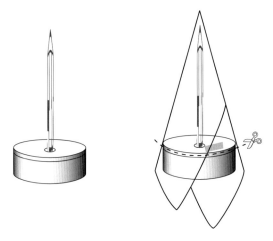

2 Bend a sheet of A4 card into a conical 'megaphone' shape to fit over the pencil; tape it together. Draw a line on the inside of

the cone where the edges of the cardboard overlap. Remove the tape, then draw another line 6mm (¼in) away from the first. Cut along the second line: this will be the overlap for gluing the cone together. Roll the card into a cone and glue together on the overlap.

3 The base of the cone will still be shaped like the sheet of cardboard that you started with. To cut it level, position the cone over the lid and cut off most of the excess card, leaving a slight overlap. Apply glue around the top edge of the lid, and to the top of the pencil. Place the cone in position and leave to dry. Carefully trim off any excess card around the base with a craft knife (see diagram, left). To hide the join line in the cardboard, glue a further two layers of thin card over it, cutting the card so that the edges butt up to one another, rather than overlapping.

Making the dome lids

1 Scrunch up aluminium foil into a ball, then flatten one side. Position the foil ball on to a lid section: the ball should not overlap the edges, as when covered in papier mâché it will form the core section of the domed lid.

2 Make up a batch of papier mâché pulp. To do this, tear up white cartridge paper into strips and then soak overnight in a bowl of warm water. Add more water to the mix and then use a blender or liquidizer to break down the paper into a pulp. Next, strain the pulp over a bowl to remove the excess water: the pulp should be damp but stiff enough to be moulded over the foil. Add PVA glue to the seived pulp, using your hands to mix it in, in the proportions of approximately 15g (½oz) glue to 250g (½lb) pulp.

3 Paint the foil with a coat of neat PVA glue. Before the glue has dried, apply the first

layer of papier mâché over the entire surface of the foil – check at regular intervals to make sure the covered foil dome is not getting too large to fit the lid section. Surface smoothness is not a priority at this stage – the idea is just to get the shape of each onion dome as well as you can. Make a tiny dome (without a foil centre) to fit on the top of the conical tower. Leave to dry in a warm place.

4 Sand the surface of each dome and then apply second coat of papier mâché, this time aiming for a smooth, even finish.

5 Position each dome on its corresponding lid section, fixing it in place with PVA and a woodscrew positioned through the hole in the centre of each disc. Glue the tiny dome on to the top of the conical tower.

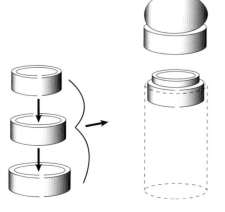

6 As they are, the lids can easily be knocked off the buildings: to keep them in place, make a lip for each lid to fit on to. To do this, cut three thin strips of cardboard that fit inside the rim of each building tube. The first strip is glued level with the rim; the second and third are fixed in position with 6mm (¼in) protruding above the rim (see diagram, below left).

Forming the base

1 Cut a piece of 2mm board approximately 20x14cm (8x5½in). Position the building tubes on to the card, leaving a gap at the front between the tubes for a note pad. Mark around each tube with a pencil, then cut the board slightly larger than the area covered by the tubes. Cut another piece of cardboard the same size and glue the two pieces together.

2 Apply two coats of white undercoat to the base, the buildings and the lids, taking care to apply it thinly over the rims and the inside edge of each lid. When the undercoat is dry, paint the base and the outside of each building tube with brick-red acrylic.

Painting the domes

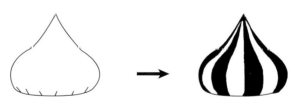

1 To paint the blue and white dome, mark a dot with a pencil at the point near the base of the dome, then mark a corresponding point on the opposite side of the dome. Keep dividing the sections in half until the dome is divided into 16 equal parts. Draw a line from each of these points to the tip of the dome. Paint the stripes with blue and white acrylic.

started. Paint in the strips with green and yellow acrylic.

2 To paint the green and yellow dome, mark points around the base as before, but this time mark 16 points around the middle of the dome as well. Join each dot at the base to a dot four points further around on the middle row, then continue the line until it joins the top of the dome on the opposite side to where it

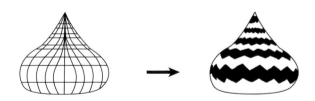

3 To paint the red and white dome, mark equally spaced dots around the dome and then draw lines from the base up to the top of the dome. Draw lines around the dome every 6mm (¼in), working up from the base to the

top. Using the grid as a guide, mark in the zigzag lines which go laterally around the dome, using a pencil. Paint using red and white gloss acrylics.

Applying the gold decoration

1 Paint the tiny dome, the tip of each painted dome and the edges of the rims and building tubes with three coats of gold metallic paint.

2 The decorative detail lines are all applied in stages. Firstly the tube rims and the horizontal lines are painted gold and white – these can be painted by resting the brush horizontally on a box and turning the tube while keeping it in contact with the brush.

When the paint is dry, add vertical lines and the arches in gold and white. Finally, using the photograph opposite for position, fill in the detail on the buildings and lids using white, red, blue and yellow.

Assembling the structure

1 Glue each tube in position on to the baseboard using PVA: hold the tubes in position until the glue is dry, and wipe away any glue that squeezes out around the edge with a damp cloth.

2 For extra protection, paint the structure inside and out with a coat of gloss varnish. When dry, add a notepad to the base, and fill with pens and pencils.

Use this plan as a guide for cutting and positioning the building tubes and rooftops. You can vary the height and size of the tubes depending on what you will be storing in them.

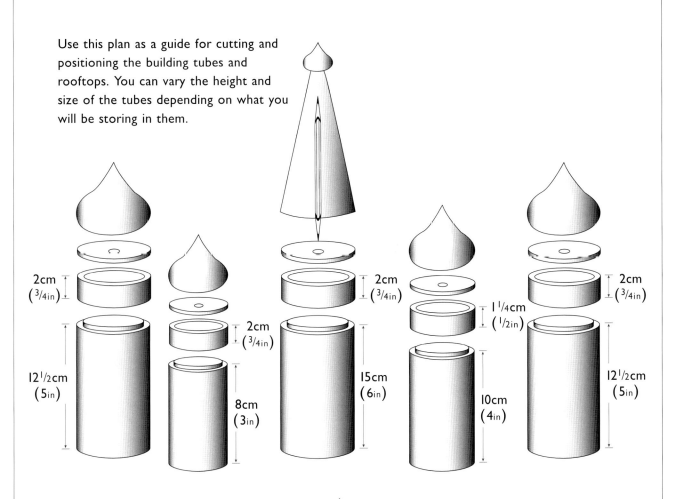

2cm (^{3}/$_4$in)

2cm (^{3}/$_4$in)

2cm (^{3}/$_4$in)

1^1/$_4$cm (^{1}/$_2$in)

2cm (^{3}/$_4$in)

12^1/$_2$cm (5in)

8cm (3in)

15cm (6in)

10cm (4in)

12^1/$_2$cm (5in)

Circus Fun Desk Set

This fun desk set is made using 3-D découpage and is ideal for a child's room. Some elements of the picture design are mounted directly on to the background, while others are layered using self-adhesive sticky pads. A box file and pen holder are decorated with clowns. (See Techniques page 20)

You will need

- Assorted crinkle card – yellow, red, blue, white, gold, pink
- Assorted thin card – yellow, deep blue, dark grey, peach, blue, pink, red, pale blue, white, green
- Stiff cardboard – 30x25cm (12x10in)
- Picture frame – 30x25cm (12x10in)
- Cardboard pot
- Empty cereal box
- Craft knife, cutting mat, small scissors
- Typewriter carbon paper, white paper
- Felt-tipped pens, pencil, ruler, ballpoint pen
- Double-sided self-adhesive sticky pads
- PVA glue, spray paint – red
- Tweezers, cocktail stick
- Star-shaped punch, black cotton

Making the background

Cut a piece of stiff cardboard to fit into the frame. Using scissors, cut a piece of green card to fit the lower two thirds of the picture, making the top edge uneven for the hills. Cut a piece of pale blue card to fit the sky area, extending the bottom edge so that it will fit down behind the hills. Glue the sky and hills on to the backing using PVA glue.

Making the templates

1 Make tracings of all the templates on pages 146–7 using white paper.

2 On some of the templates, like the clouds, it will be possible to cut out the tracing, lay it on the card and draw around the outside edge.

3 For the more detailed shapes, lay carbon paper on top of the card, ink side down, then over this lay the tracing. Carefully go over the lines with a ballpoint pen. This will leave a line on the card which can be cut out using either a craft knife or small scissors.

Making trees and clouds

1 Make tracings of the trees, clouds and sun. From white crinkle card cut the clouds; use yellow for the sun and gold for the trees. Arrange on the background of green and blue card, then carefully glue in position using PVA glue.

2 Make a template of the tent. Cut some parts from the red crinkle card and some from the white, using the photograph above as a guide; the flag is cut from dark blue crinkle card. Glue on to the background using PVA glue.

Making the vehicles

1 Make tracings of the lorry and trailer. From dark blue crinkle card cut out the lorry. Using a star punch, make a selection of stars from yellow, white and pink crinkle card. Glue the stars on to the lorry, and then the lorry on to the background. Cut out circles from yellow crinkle card for the lorry wheels, and glue them in position on the lorry. Cut the trailer from pink crinkle card and the wheels from blue. Do not fix the trailer in place at this stage of the project.

Making the ringmaster

1 Make tracings of the ringmaster parts. Now cut his shirt from red card. Use a black felt-tipped pen to add a collar, buttons and cuff.

Cut two faces from peach card and two hats from grey; add detail to one face and one hat using felt-tipped pens. Glue the ringmaster's shirt inside the window opening of the lorry and on to this glue the unmarked head and hat (the hat should slightly overlap the face). Cut self-adhesive sticky pads into small pieces, peel off the backing paper, and attach them to the centre of the face and hat using tweezers. Position the decorated face and hat on to the pads, making sure they are exactly over the shapes beneath. Cut out one hand from peach card and glue it under the end of the sleeve.

Making the small clown

1 Cut two body shapes for the small clown from pink card. On one shape add spots and stripes using felt-tipped pens.

2 Cut two faces and four hands from peach card; add the features to one face using felt-tipped pens. Cut out two hat shapes and four shoes from bright blue card.

3 Stick the undecorated clown's body, feet, hands, face and hat on to the background using PVA glue, slightly overlapping the pieces. Cover the clown with small pieces of self-adhesive sticky pad, then carefully position the decorated pieces on top, making sure that they are directly over the pieces beneath. Add small circles of silver paper to the clown's hat, and glue hair made from short lengths of yellow crinkle card on either side of the face.

4 Cut out three balloons from crinkle card, and cut three short lengths of black cotton. Use a cocktail stick to press the cotton on to tiny blobs of PVA glue, then glue the balloons to the end of the cotton.

Making the large clown

1 Cut out two coats and four shoes from blue card, two pairs of trousers from pink card, two hats from yellow card, two faces and four hands from peach card and hair from red crinkle card. Decorate one set of parts with felt-tipped pens.

2 Use PVA glue to attach the base layer, and pieces of self-adhesive sticky pad to attach the decorated layer over the base. Add three balloons in the same way as for the small clown.

Making the elephant

1 Cut the elephant's body pieces, head and ear from dark grey card, and the blanket and headdress from pink card; from white card cut four small squares for the elephant's toenails, two small triangles for his eyes and two triangles for his tusks. With felt-tipped pens, add shading to the ear and trunk. Use PVA glue to attach the base layer and pieces of self-adhesive sticky pad to attach the second layer, adding the blanket with glue. Use the sticky pads to attach the head, adding the eyes and tusks with glue, then attach the ear on sticky pads.

Making the lion

1 Cut the lion pieces from yellow card, adding detail to the mane and body using felt-tipped pens.

2 Using sticky pads attach the mane and face to the lion's body. Weave the lion's body through the bars of the trailer, leaving his head protruding out. Fix the lion and the trailer behind the lorry, adding two circles of blue crinkle card for the wheels.

Making the seals

1 From dark grey card cut out the first seal's body parts, flipping the templates for the second seal; add shading with a black felt-tipped pen. Glue the base layer with PVA, then add the body and flippers on sticky pads. From the yellow and red crinkle card, cut out a ball shape. Glue the ball above one seal on the background. Use small pieces of black cotton for the seals' whiskers.

Making the grass

1 Cut spiky tufts of grass from gold crinkle card and glue along the front edge of the picture. Decorate with small flower shapes cut from pink and yellow crinkle card.

Making the box and pen pot

1 Cut the top from a cereal box, then cut away the sides at an angle. Glue pale green card on to the inside surface of the box, and yellow crinkle card on the outside. Punch stars from coloured card and glue them around the edge of the box. Enlarge the clown trace on a photocopier to fit the box. Cut out the pieces, then attach them to the side of the box, making them up in the same way as for the picture.

2 Spray or paint a cardboard pot inside and out with red paint. Attach a large and small clown to the side of the pot.

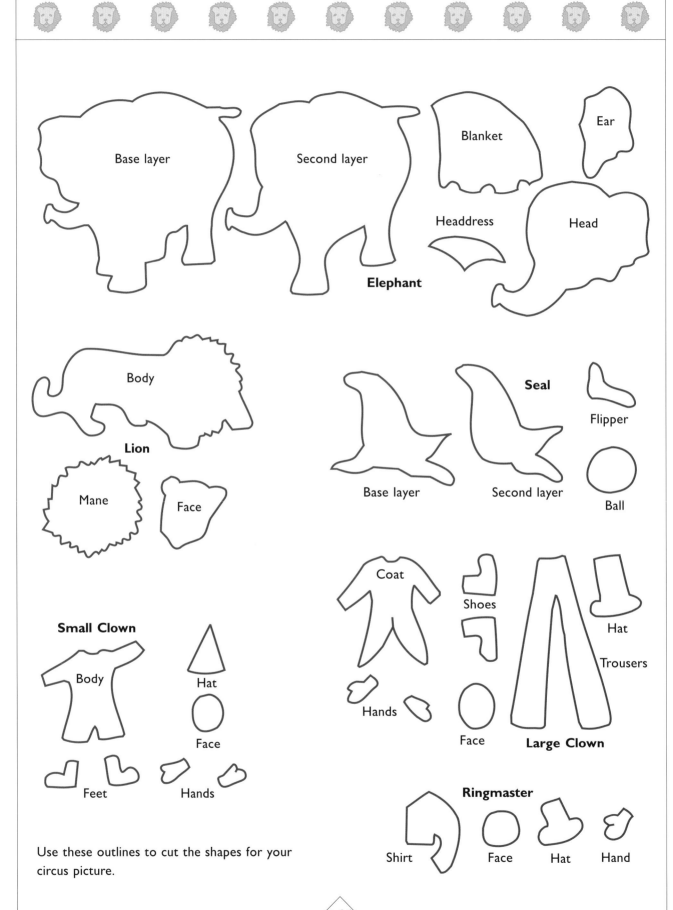

Base layer

Second layer

Blanket

Ear

Headdress

Head

Elephant

Body

Lion

Mane

Face

Seal

Base layer

Second layer

Flipper

Ball

Coat

Shoes

Hat

Trousers

Small Clown

Body

Hat

Face

Hands

Face

Large Clown

Feet

Hands

Ringmaster

Shirt

Face

Hat

Hand

Use these outlines to cut the shapes for your circus picture.

Petal and Leaf Writing Set

Potpourri and pressed flowers have been used as an ingredient in the
paper-making process, giving this stationery set texture as well as scent.
For an autumnal feel, the set is finished with plaits and tassels made from
thick embroidery thread. (See Techniques page 10)

You will need

- Stationery box
- Address book
- Paper for making pulp
- Dried leaves and flowers
- Potpourri
- Thin card
- Cardboard tube
- Wool or thick embroidery thread
- Mould and deckle
- Bucket, length of wood or hand-held liquidizer
- Plastic tray to use as a vat
- Kitchen cloths, rectangle of hardboard
- Newspaper
- Clean bricks or heavy weights
- Craft knife and cutting mat, scissors
- Tacky glue, masking tape, water

Making coloured paper

1 Prepare the paper pulp (see Making a Sheet of Paper, page 13). Recycle only light-coloured paper for this project. Beige-coloured envelopes and paper bags can also be used, as long as the colour is not too strong (see Making Pulp, page 11).

2 For this project you will need to make three different types of paper: natural, potpourri textured, and some decorated with dried flowers and leaves.

3 Using the prepared paper pulp, make one sheet of natural-coloured paper as described in Making a Sheet of Paper, pages 13–16.

4 Add more water and pulp to the vat, being careful to keep the ratio of pulp to water the same as when you started. Give the pulp a good stir and then drop dried flower petals and leaves on to the surface of the pulp (see Making Decorative Paper, page 17). You can dry your own petals and leaves by pressing them between the pages of a heavy book for several weeks, or they can be bought from a craft shop.

5 Make four sheets of petal and leaf paper. Although you will not use all four sheets to cover the stationery box, you will be able to choose the parts of the paper with the best concentration of petals and leaves.

6 Remove any petals or leaves that are still on the surface of the pulp, and then top up the vat with pulp and water.

7 Put a good handful of potpourri into a paper bag, seal the top and then crush the potpourri into very small pieces.

8 Sprinkle crushed potpourri pieces into the vat, and give the pulp a good stir. Keep adding potpourri and stirring until you are happy that it is evenly spread throughout the pulp.

9 Make four sheets of paper in the same way as before, using the potpourri pulp.

Covering the stationery box

1 Buy a stationery box with a drawer and lift-up lid. Remove the drawer and cover its front with petal and leaf paper, and the sides with natural paper: use natural paper in places where the paper needs to be flatter.

2 Using wool or thick embroidery thread, make a short plait. Knot one end together to stop it unravelling, and apply glue to the

other. Glue the plait to the underside of the drawer. Cover the base of the drawer with natural paper.

3 Make another plait to go between the lid and the top of the box. Glue the plait in place, and then cover the box in the same way as the drawer. Try to cut the paper so that the best petals and leaves are positioned prominently on the box.

4 Strengthen the join between the lid and the box with a strip of natural paper, glued along the hinge between the two parts.

5 Put the drawer back in the box. Make two bundles of stationery and tie them up with lengths of wool. Place one bundle in the drawer, and the other in the recess at the top of the box.

Covering the address book

1 Cut a piece of potpourri paper so it is slightly larger than the cover of the book. Glue the paper on to the front and back cover. Make a small cut in the excess paper either side of the spine, top and bottom; add glue to the flaps of

paper, and then push them down between the spine of the book. Glue the excess paper at the edges on to the inside of the covers.

2 Tear a leaf roughly out of the petal and leaf paper, and glue it to the front of the book. Make a long plait of wool or embroidery thread, loop it over the top of the book, and then glue it down the folds on the front and back, where the spine and cover meet. Knot the ends together at the bottom.

Making the bookmark

1 Cut two rectangles of thin card 4x15cm (1½x6in). Cover one side of each rectangle with potpourri paper.

2 Cut thirty 10cm (4in) lengths of wool to make the tassel. Fold these over a longer

length of wool. Tie the bunch together, 4cm (1½in) from the folded ends.

3 Glue the rectangles of paper-covered card together, with the tassel ends between the two cards, and the tassel protruding at one end of the bookmark. Glue a single strand of wool around the edge, pushing the ends between the card layers. Decorate the bookmark with a torn leaf in the same way as for the book.

Making the basket

1 Cut 4cm (1½in) from an empty cardboard tube. Cut a circle of card for the base, and a card strip for the basket handle. Glue in place, then cover the joins with masking tape.

2 Cover the basket, inside and out, with petal and leaf paper, and then fill with potpourri.

Scrap Paper Photo Albums

These photo albums are covered with wonderfully textured handmade paper created by adding thread, fabric, ribbon, wool, beads and sequins to the paper pulp. In addition, pulses, like split peas and lentils, make interesting effects. The photograph albums are easy to make, and are useful as well as attractive. (See Techniques page 10)

You will need

- A2 card – silver
- Small pieces of wool, ribbon, material, beads, lentils, small ribbon rosebuds
- Silver ribbon for the leporello ties
- Stiff card for the album covers
- Thin frosted plastic cut from a video cover
- Hole punch, two metal screwbinders
- Stiff paper for album pages and spacers – white
- Paper for making pulp
- Mould and deckle
- Bucket, length of wood or hand-held liquidizer
- Newspaper, rectangles of hardboard
- Clean bricks or heavy weights
- Scissors, rolling pin, screwdriver
- Tacky glue, kitchen cloths, water
- Craft knife and cutting mat
- Pencil, ruler

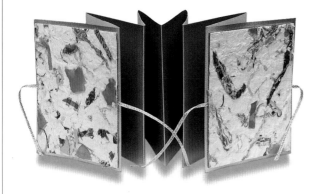

Making the scrap paper

1 Choose light-coloured paper with long fibres for this project (see Making Pulp, page 11). Tear the paper into small squares about the size of a postage stamp. Put the torn paper into a bucket, cover with cold water and leave to soak for several days (see Making a Sheet of Paper, page 13). You will need to top up the water as it gets drawn into the paper.

2 When the paper has been well soaked, pour away any water that remains. Using a hand-held liquidizer or a piece of wood, beat the paper until it is a smooth, creamy consistency.

3 Half fill a plastic tray with water. Put pulp into the tray so that there is a ratio of approximately one third pulp to two thirds water. Stir the pulp and water together.

4 Cover your work surface with plenty of newspaper. Place a folded pad of newspaper in the centre, and on top of this a piece of hardboard and a folded kitchen cloth.

5 Give the pulp another good stir. Place the deckle on top of the mould, with the net side uppermost and lining up the edges exactly.

6 Sprinkle small pieces of thread, wool, ribbon, material and beads on to the surface of the pulp in shades that work well

together. Ribbon roses and dried pulses like lentil can also be added to the pulp. Do not stir the pulp at this stage.

7 Holding the mould and deckle firmly together, push it into the pulp (see Making a Sheet of Paper, page 14), making sure you scoop up the threads and materials floating on the pulp. Straighten up the mould and deckle just below the surface of the pulp. Gently lift, letting the excess water drain back into the vat. Remove the deckle from the mould.

8 Turn the mould over so that the paper is upside down under the mould: the wet net will hold the paper firmly in place. In one gentle movement, transfer the wet sheet of paper on to the kitchen cloth. Press down on one short edge of the mould, then lift up the opposite edge, leaving the paper on the cloth.

9 Make a stack of at least three pieces of paper, laying a folded cloth between each one. Put heavy weights on the stack for several hours to squeeze out the excess water.

10 Cover your work surface with a sheet of plastic, and then a layer of newspaper. Remove each kitchen cloth with its sheet of paper from the stack and spread them out on the plastic. Leave the paper until almost dry; this may take several hours.

11 Roll each sheet of paper with a rolling pin to give it a nice even finish. Dry the individual sheets of paper under heavy weights.

Making the leporello

1 Cut three pieces of silver card 18x56cm (7¼x22in). Using a pencil and ruler, divide the strips equally into four sections. Use the back of a knife to score along your pencil lines. Concertina-fold the strips along these lines.

Glue the strips together to make one long folded strip. Leave it to dry.

2 Cut two pieces of the handmade paper 13x17cm (5¼x6¾in). Cut two pieces of stiff card to the same size and glue the handmade paper to the card.

3 Cut two 45cm (17¾in) lengths of silver ribbon. Glue one length horizontally across the middle of the front cover of the leporello, and one across the back.

4 Glue one of the card-backed pieces of handmade paper on to the front of the leporello and one on to the back. This will hold the ribbon firmly in place.

5 Fold up the leporello, tying the ribbon ends together to keep it closed. Press between heavy weights and leave to dry overnight.

Making the photo album

1 Choose two pieces of handmade paper for the front and back covers. Cut them to approximately 17x19cm (6¾x7½in). If you wish, you may tear the edges to give a natural

effect. To do this, first fold and then dampen the paper with water before tearing.

2 Cut two pieces of stiff card just smaller than the paper – these are the covers on to which the handmade paper is attached. On one cover draw a pencil line 2.5cm (1in) in from the left-hand edge. Score along this line with a ruler and the back of a scalpel. This will form the hinge for the front cover of the album.

3 Glue the pieces of handmade paper to the card covers. Place the assembled covers between clean card and put them under a heavy weight until the glue is dry.

4 Cut two pieces of the silver card 2.5x17cm (1x6³⁄₄in), and two of frosted plastic from a video cover. These pieces will cover and protect the spine on the front and back cover.

5 For the album pages, cut sheets of stiff white paper 16x18cm (6¹⁄₄x7in). Score a line

2.5cm (1in) in along the left-hand edge. Cut six pieces of stiff paper 2.5x16cm (1x6¹⁄₄in) – these strips of paper will be placed between the pages of the album to act as spacers.

6 Punch holes in the spine pieces, covers, pages and spacers, making sure that all the holes will line up when the album is finally assembled.

Assembling the album

1 Using a screwdriver, undo the two screwbinders – a screwbinder is made up of two metal parts that screw together, and extra metal spacers that can be added as you need to extend the pages in your album. Assemble the album, pushing the screwbinders through the two holes in the album parts. Start from the front with the frosted plastic spine, then the silver card spine, front cover, album pages with spacers between, back cover, silver card spine, and finally the back frosted plastic spine. Screw the back on the screwbinder.

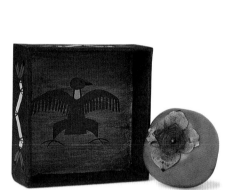

DECORATIVE ITEMS

It is surprising how versatile paper is – it can be used to embellish, cover, strengthen and even as a design tool itself. This collection of decorative items will delight anyone looking to make something substantial and functional from paper, whether to use in their own home or as a gift for a loved one.

★ **Spiral Stamps** (page 158) are a simple but stylish way to brighten up pots, greetings cards and anything else you like, using corrugated card and string.

★ **Native American Trays** (page 160), constructed from cardboard and papier mâché, are finished with leather thonging and beads, and will lend an ethnic feel to any décor.

★ **Embellished Rose Casket** (page 164) is covered in papier mâché for strength and texture. Once decorated, it has a sumptuous appearance, and could be given as a gift with the matching card.

★ **Geometric Trinket Boxes** (page 172) are a stylish way of organizing your trinkets, with paste-decorated, handmade paper transforming shoe boxes into storage you won't want to hide!

★ **Botanical Picture and Box** (page 176) make perfect gifts for a green-fingered friend. 3-D découpage transforms floral gift-wrap into decorative botanical specimens.

★ **Marbled Frame** (page 182), made from paper marbled with colourful oil paints, allows you to display a favourite photo or make the daisy flowers to fit inside.

Spiral Stamps

If you have ever wondered what to do with the paint left over from a decorating spree, then this is the project for you. Alternatively, you can buy tester pots of paint, which will give you enough paint for a few terracotta pots and a selection of greetings cards. (See Techniques pages 44 and 28)

You will need

- For the pots: terracotta plant pots
- For the cards: coloured card – green, blue, yellow; textured paper – green, yellow, pink
- Emulsion paint – green, blue, yellow, pink
- Thick string, corrugated card
- Craft knife, cutting board, scissors, ruler
- All-purpose glue
- Paintbrush
- Pencil, ballpoint pen

Preparing the pots

1 Wash the pots to remove any dust or marks, then allow to dry. Paint the pots with two coats of emulsion paint. Leave to dry.

Preparing the stamps

1 Draw a freehand spiral and coil on to corrugated card, or use a pencil to trace the outlines opposite on to white paper. Lay the tracing on top of corrugated card, then draw over the lines with a ballpoint pen, transferring them to the card. Glue along the design lines on the card, then lay string over the glue. Cut off the excess string. Cut the card around the outer edge of the string design, leaving a 6mm (¹⁄₄in) margin.

Stamping the pot and paper

1 Paint the top of the string liberally with emulsion paint, then press firmly on to the pot. Stamp the textured paper in the same way. Leave to dry.

Assembling the greetings card

1 To achieve the torn edge effect on the textured paper, hold a ruler firmly on the paper at one side of the design and tear away the excess paper. Repeat on the other sides.

2 Fold a piece of coloured card in half to make a card. Glue the textured paper to the front of the card.

Native American Trays

Brown paper papier mâché strips form the basis of these rectangular trays. Clever use of painted geometric shapes, arrows, birds and feathers, together with beads and leather thongs, produce an authentic effect. (See Techniques page 36)

You will need
- Corrugated card
- Newspaper
- Acrylic paint – cream, dark red, black and turquoise
- Masking tape
- Brown parcel paper, white paper, ballpoint pen, typewriter carbon paper
- PVA glue, water, container for mixing glue
- Bradawl, glue brush, paintbrush
- Water-based acrylic matt varnish
- Turquoise leather thonging
- Beads

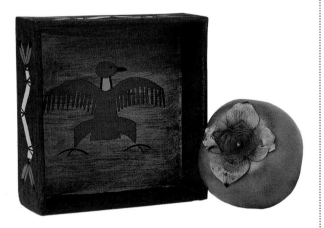

Making the large tray

1 For the large tray, cut out a rectangle of corrugated card 35.5x25cm (14x10in) in dimension, and four strips of corrugated card that measures 35.5x4.5cm (14x1¾in).

2 Using masking tape, attach two of the strips upright against the long sides of the large rectangle. Tape the remaining two strips against the shorter edges of the card, cutting their ends level with the ends of the first strips to form the sides of the tray. Tape the corners together using masking tape.

Applying the papier mâché

1 Tear the newspaper into 5cm (2in) strips. Mix the PVA glue in a container with a little water until it is the consistency of single cream.

2 Brush the PVA solution on to a newspaper strip and smooth it over the tray. Continue adding strips, overlapping the edges of the paper, until you have built up 10 layers: each layer should be laid in a different direction. To strengthen the corners, tear the newspaper into smaller strips and paste them smoothly around the corners.

3 Apply a final layer of brown parcel paper strips over the entire surface of the tray, then leave to dry: this may take several days.

Use a bradawl to make a row of holes on
the sides of the tray, equidistant apart and
1cm (⅜in) below the upper edge – approximately
four holes on the short side and seven holes on the
long side.

Painting the large tray

1 Thin the cream paint with a little water,
then paint the base and underside of the
tray, giving it a streaky finish. Thin the dark
red paint in the same way, then paint the sides
of the tray, inside and out.

2 Make a tracing of the large, geometric
design opposite on to white paper. Lay the
typewriter carbon paper over half of the tray,
shiny side down. Lay the tracing on top, then
carefully draw over the design lines, transferring
them to the tray. Turn the tracing around and
repeat for the other half of the tray, making
sure the two halves are matched up.

3 Paint the design in black, cream, dark red
and turquoise, following the photograph for
position. Leave to dry.

4 Paint the tray with three coats of acrylic
varnish for protection.

5 When dry, lace the thonging through the
holes, adding beads randomly. Knot the

thong ends together, thread a bead on each end
and then knot together again.

Making the small tray

1 For the small tray, cut a 10cm (4in) square
of corrugated card, two strips 10x3cm
(4x1¼in) and two 12x3cm (5x1¼in).

2 Tape the four strips on to the sides of the
cardboard square, cutting the ends level at
the corners to form the sides of the tray. Then
tape the corners together using masking tape.

3 Apply layers of newspaper and brown paper
in the same way as for the large tray.

4 Thin the cream paint with water, then
paint the base and underside of the tray,
giving it a streaky finish. Paint the sides with
thinned dark red paint and allow to dry.

5 Make a tracing of the bird motif below and
the feather motif opposite. Use carbon paper
to transfer the design lines to the tray as for the
large tray: the bird on the base and a feather
motif on the outside of each side. Paint the
bird and feather motifs in turquoise, black,
cream and dark red, following the photograph
for position. Allow to dry, then apply three coats
of acrylic varnish to the tray for protection.

Bird motif

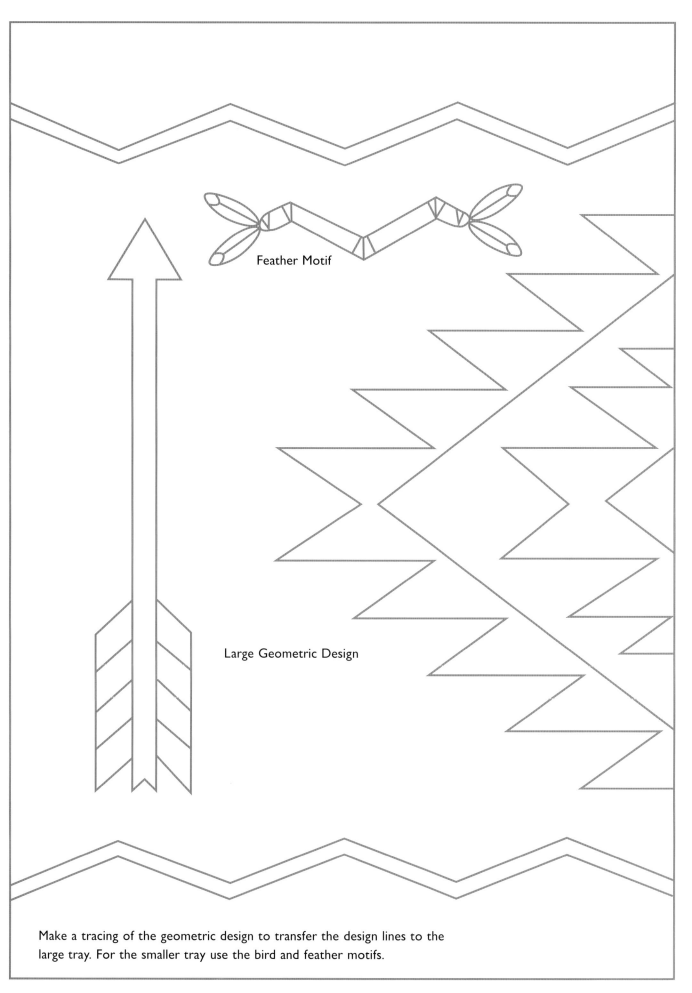

Feather Motif

Large Geometric Design

Make a tracing of the geometric design to transfer the design lines to the large tray. For the smaller tray use the bird and feather motifs.

Embellished Rose Casket

This papier mâché casket would make a wonderful Valentine or anniversary gift, or you may prefer to make just the roses and use them to create a special card or gift tag. To give the casket an extra special finish, add gold braid, beads and small brass charms. (See Techniques page 36)

You will need

- Stiff mounting board – 30x55cm (12x22in)
- Ready-mixed papier mâché pulp
- Gift-wrap tissue paper – purple, blue, pink, red, gold
- Newspaper, aluminium baking foil
- Stiff card – gold
- Emulsion paint – white
- Acrylic paint – gold, burgundy, deep red, green
- Plastic sweet moulds – hearts, roses
- Greetings card, parcel label
- Narrow braid – gold
- Small gold charms, gold thread, beads, needle
- PVA glue, water, washing-up liquid
- Scissors, pencil, white paper
- Masking tape, blunt knife, sandpaper
- Glue brush, paintbrushes
- Container for mixing glue
- Water-based matt acrylic varnish

Making the hearts and roses

1 Make a quantity of papier mâché using ready-mixed paper pulp or make your own paper pulp (see Making Paper Pulp page 38).

2 Rub the inside of the heart and rose sweet moulds with neat washing-up liquid to prevent the papier mâché sticking to the plastic.

3 Press a small quantity of pulp into the mould. Turn the mould over to check that the shape is filled with pulp and there are no air baubles. Keep adding lumps of pulp until the mould is filled, smooth the surface, then leave to dry for several days.

4 When the papier mâché shapes are completely dry, they will shrink away from the edges of

the mould, and can be tipped out. Neaten the edges of each shape with scissors or a knife, then rub the back on sandpaper to make a flat surface for attaching to the casket.

Painting the hearts and roses

1 Apply two coats of red paint to the hearts and roses. Paint the leaves on the roses green and then add detail to the rose petals using burgundy paint. Allow to dry, then highlight some areas with gold paint in order to emphasize the shape.

Making the casket

1 Using white paper, trace over the templates for the casket on the following four pages.

2 Cut out the templates then lay them on to a sheet of mounting board; trace around the edges with a pencil. Cut the number of pieces indicated in each template: when assembled they will form a casket and lid.

Forming the casket

1 Take the front section and one side of the casket and fix together with small strips of masking tape. Make the other side and the back in the same way. Once you have assembled the rectangular box, reinforce the corners with lengths of masking tape.

2 Measure 1.2cm (½in) in from the edges of the base and draw a rectangle in pencil: this is a guide for fixing the casket sides.

3 Apply PVA glue along the bottom edge of the rectangular box and place it centrally on to the base: use your pencil line to make sure the box is in position. Hold the two sections firmly together, then leave to dry for an hour.

4 Glue the two long insert strips along the inside of the front and back edges of the

casket, with 1.2cm (½in) protruding above the top of the sides: this will give a ledge for the lid to sit over. Repeat for the two shorter sides.

Making the lid

1 Using the templates on the following pages, cut the lid and lid ends from mounting board. Score the lid in the places marked by the dotted lines using a blunt knife; fold on the scored lines.

2 Apply a layer of PVA glue along the top edge of one lid end-piece. Place the scored and folded lid over the lid end, holding it in place with strips of masking tape. Repeat for the other side, then check that the lid fits before leaving it to dry.

Applying the papier mâché

1 Tear strips of newspaper into 4x2cm (1½x¾in) pieces. Mix equal quantities of PVA glue and water in a container.

2 Brush the PVA glue mix on to a small area on the outside of the casket. Place a piece of newspaper over the glued area then brush over with more glue, removing any bubbles or creases that appear. Add more newspaper pieces,

overlapping the edges until the outside of the casket base is covered. Press the paper firmly around the rim of the casket; this ensures that the lid will fit. Do the same for the inside and the outside of the lid, and then leave the lid and base to dry overnight.

3 Cut four 10cm (4in) squares of aluminium foil and scrunch into balls. Turn the casket upside down and apply circles of PVA glue 2.5cm (1in) from each corner on the base. Press a foil ball on to each glue circle to make feet.

4 Apply a second layer of papier mâché strips over the casket, the foil feet and the lid.

5 When dry, paint the inside and outside of the casket and lid with white emulsion, then leave to dry.

Applying the tissue paper

1 Cut the tissue gift-wrap into the diamond shapes using the diamond tissue template.

2 Mix equal quantities of PVA glue and water in a container, then brush a thin coat onto one side of the casket; apply a tissue diamond over the glue. Brush on more PVA and position another diamond partly covering the first; as you work, use the brush to smooth out any air bubbles that may have appeared under the tissue.

Be careful, as the wet tissue paper can stick to your fingers and pull off the casket. If necessary work on very small sections, leaving the tissue to dry for an hour before adding more diamonds. Keep adding the tissue until the surface of the lid and casket are covered: the tissue paper should go inside the casket but no lower than the rim inserts. Leave to dry overnight.

3 If any of the diamond edges hve become unstuck refix with a tiny amount of PVA glue. Allow to dry, then apply three coats of matt acrylic varnish for protection.

4 Using the templates for the decorative panels, carefully cut out two small and three large panels from gold tissue paper. Then secure a small panel on to each side of the casket, and a large panel on to the front, back and lid using PVA glue.

5 With an almost dry brush, highlight the edges of the casket with gold acrylic paint.

6 Using PVA glue, fix a length of gold braid around the bottom of the lid. Thread a needle with fine gold thread and attach beads and charms to the braids at the corners and the midway points.

7 Glue a painted heart in the centre of each gold tissue panel.

Making the card and gift tag

1 Cut a circle of gold card larger than your papier mâché rose. Glue the gold circle to the front of the greetings card, then edge the circle with gold braid. Stick the painted rose on to the centre of the circle using PVA glue.

2 To make a gift tag, glue a painted rose on to a parcel label, then thread with gold ribbon.

Casket Front/Back
– cut 2

Casket Lid
– cut 1

Diamond
Tissue
Template

Casket Front/Back Insert
– cut 2

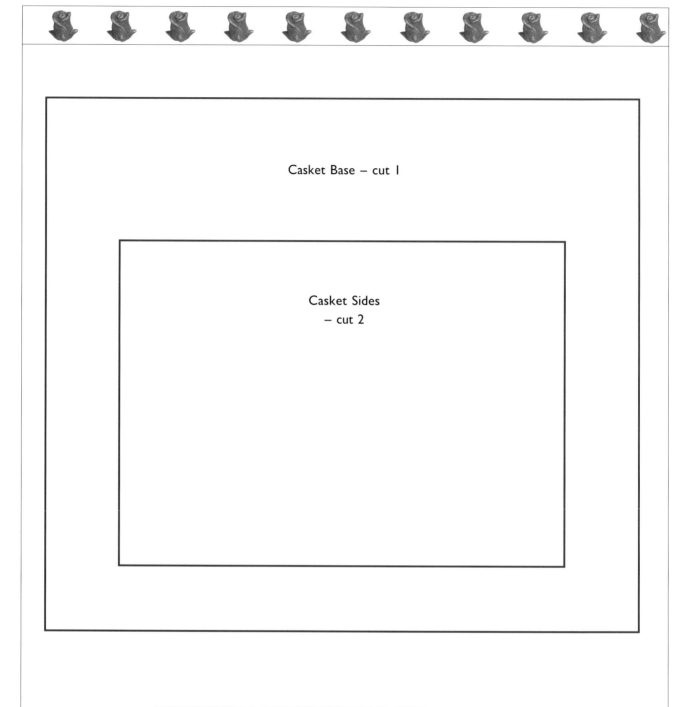

Casket Base – cut 1

Casket Sides
– cut 2

Casket Lid
End – cut 2

Casket Side Insert – cut 1

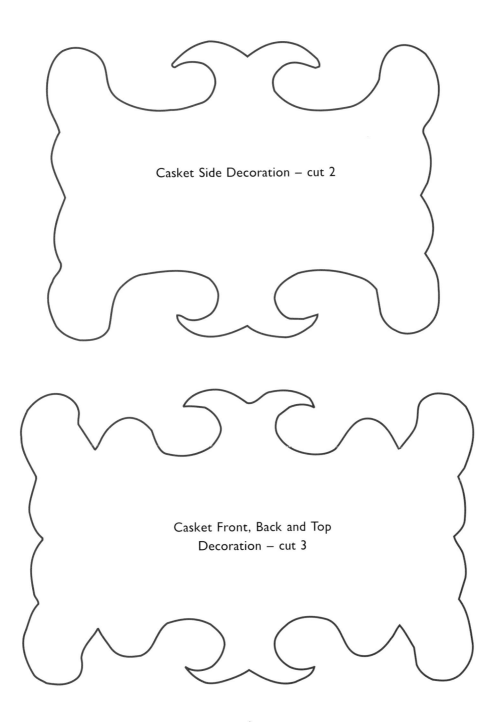

Casket Side Decoration – cut 2

Casket Front, Back and Top
Decoration – cut 3

Geometric Trinket Boxes

Geometric designs painted in fresh colours on handmade paper have been used to turn these plain cardboard shoe boxes into a set of stylish storage boxes. The designs are made by using a combination of wallpaper paste and paint, while the paper is made from recycled envelopes and computer print-out paper. (See Techniques page 10)

You will need

- Shoe boxes
- Paper for making pulp
- Wallpaper paste
- Acrylic paint – apple green, turquoise, lavender
- Food colouring – cerise
- Cream card and raffia for making tags
- Mould and deckle
- Bucket, length of wood or hand-held liquidizer
- Plastic tray to use as a vat
- Kitchen cloths, rectangle of hardboard
- Newspaper
- Clean bricks or heavy weights
- Rolling pin
- Mixing bowl
- Hole punch
- Paintbrushes – large and small
- Craft knife and cutting mat, scissors
- Tacky glue, water

Making paper pulp

1 Make a mould and deckle following the instructions on page 12. Recycle only light-coloured paper for this project – computer print-out paper, paper bags and envelopes all have long fibres and will make strong paper. Avoid coloured or printed paper as you may find it difficult to cover the resulting surface colour with paint. Do not use paper with a shiny surface as it may be coated with clay, which will leave powdery patches on the finished paper (see Making Pulp, page 11).

2 Look over the paper to be recycled; discard any covered with glue and take out staples. Tear the paper into small squares, about the size of a postage stamp.

3 Put the torn paper in a bucket, cover with cold water and leave to soak for several days. You will need to top up the water as it gets drawn into the paper.

4 When the paper has been well soaked, pour away any water that remains. Using a hand-held liquidizer or a piece of wood, beat the paper to a mushy pulp. This will take quite a long time as the pulp needs to be very smooth and creamy.

5 Half fill a plastic tray with water. Pour pulp into the tray so that there is a ratio of

approximately one third pulp to two thirds water. Stir the pulp and water together.

6 The wet sheets of paper will hold a great deal of water, so it is important to cover your work surface with newspaper. Place a folded pad of newspaper in the centre, and on top of this a piece of hardboard and a wet kitchen cloth.

7 Give the pulp another good stir. Place the deckle on top of the mould, with the net side uppermost and lining up the edges exactly. Press the pieces firmly together.

Making a sheet of paper

1 Push the mould and deckle into the pulp. Straighten up the mould and deckle just below the surface of the pulp. Gently lift, letting the excess water drain back into the vat. Remove the deckle from the mould. For more details, see Making a Sheet of Paper pages 13–16.

2 Turn the mould over so that the paper is upside down under the mould: the wet net will hold the paper firmly in place. In one gentle movement, transfer the wet sheet of paper to the kitchen cloth. Press down on one short edge of the mould, and then lift up the opposite end, leaving the paper on the cloth.

3 Make a stack of five sheets of paper, laying a wet kitchen cloth between each one. Cover the stack with a heavy weight for several hours to press out some of the water.

4 Cover your work surface with a sheet of plastic, and then a layer of newspaper. Remove each kitchen cloth with its sheet of paper from the stack and spread them out over the protected surface. Leave until almost dry; this will take several hours.

5 To give the paper a smooth surface, roll each sheet with a rolling pin while it is still damp. To keep the paper flat, dry the sheets separately under a weighted board. Make enough sheets to cover your set of boxes.

Decorating the paper

1 Mix wallpaper paste with water to the consistency recommended for hanging lightweight wallpaper. Leave the paste to set overnight. Cover your working area with a thick layer of clean newspaper.

2 Lay a sheet of handmade paper on to the newspaper and paint a generous layer of paste over the sheet.

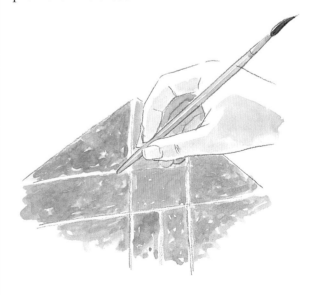

3 Apply apple green and turquoise or lavender and turquoise acrylic paint in random blobs onto the paste. Blend the colours together where they meet, using a soft paintbrush.

4 Make diamond shapes over the surface of the paper, using the blunt end of a paintbrush to draw lines in the wet paste. Using the designs opposite as a guide, draw freehand cherry and pear shapes within the larger diamond, and swirls in the smaller ones. Do not press too hard or the paper may tear.

5 Carefully arrange each sheet of paper to dry, laying them on a clothes horse or over the slats in an airing cupboard. Depending on the thickness of the paste, the sheets will take between 4–6 hours to dry. Paint enough sheets to cover your boxes.

6 If the paper has wrinkled, flatten each sheet under a heavy weight and leave overnight.

Decorating the boxes

1 Apply a thin, even layer of tacky glue to the outer surface of the box. Cover the box using the sheets of decorated paper, smoothing each one flat to remove air bubbles. If the box is larger than the size of the paper, use several sheets, overlapping the edges where they meet.

2 Line the inside of the box with bright pink handmade paper. Refer to the instructions for making coloured paper on pages 10 and 17.

Making a tag

1 Tags can be made using small scraps of decorated paper glued to a rectangle of cream card. Punch two evenly spaced holes at the top edge of the tag. Thread with natural-coloured raffia, and then attach to the box. Write the contents of the box on the tag for easy reference.

Use these outlines to draw freehand fruit shapes on to your boxes.

Botanical Picture and Box

This botanical picture and pretty gift box and tag have been created using floral gift-wrap. Use paper with clear images and well defined edges. When shaped and layered in 3-D découpage the flowers look like specimens torn from the pages of a botanical notebook. (See Techniques page 20)

Choose gift-wrap that has at least six copies of the same illustration; alternatively, buy several sheets of the same paper.

You will need

● Floral gift-wrap with repeat design and border
● Silicone glue, cocktail stick, tweezers
● Wooden box frame
● Thick card – cream
● Craft knife, cutting mat, scissors
● Fine sandpaper
● Acrylic paint – red
● Handmade or textured paper
● Paper glue or spray adhesive, blunt knife
● 3-D découpage shaping mat and tool, or spoon
● Double-sided sticky tape
● Hole punch
● Paintbrush

Building layers

1 Silicone is a clear glue-like substance that is used to hold the layers of the picture in position. You can also build the layers using self-adhesive sticky pads. However, for a small detailed design like the flowers opposite, silicone is more flexible.

2 Although the silicone container has a fine nozzle and can be used straight from the tube, it is much easier to apply using a cocktail stick. Apply blobs of silicone between 2mm (¹/₁₆in) and 5mm (¹/₄in) high on to the fixed layer, not to the back of the paper piece being applied; position a blob roughly in the centre, and if needed smaller blobs closer to the edges. Keep the silicone well away from the outer edges of the paper or it will show in your finished picture, and avoid getting it on your fingers as this will make handling the paper pieces very difficult. Do not start applying the silicone until you have cut the next paper layer, or it may dry before you can position the paper.

3 Use tweezers to position the paper pieces on to the silicone, and a cocktail stick to nudge the paper gently into position. Do not press hard on the paper pieces, as this may spread the silicone and flatten the layers beneath. Make sure that each piece is directly over the picture beneath: this is important as the overall effect will be spoiled if the layers are not in line.

Preparing the frame

1 Lightly sand the box frame, then wipe over with a damp cloth to remove any dust. Pick up a little red acrylic paint on to a paintbrush and then drag the paint around the frame working in one direction. Leave to dry.

2 Check that the gift-wrap border will fit into the frame; if it is too large you will need to shorten each side when you cut it out. Tear a rectangle of handmade or textured paper 6mm (1/4in) wider on all sides than the border. To do this, tear the paper against a ruler (see page 31).

3 Remove the board back from the frame; stick a layer of cream paper over the board, and then the torn paper centrally on top using glue or spray adhesive.

Cutting out the border

1 On a cutting mat and using a sharp craft knife, cut the border from the gift-wrap. Make sure your craft knife blade is very sharp; if you use a blunt blade you may damage the print. You can also use small embroidery scissors for cutting the larger shapes.

2 Using glue or spray adhesive, attach the border to the background paper: this is the base layer.

3 Cut out the second border layer, exactly the same as the base layer. Position it over the base layer on small blobs of silicone. When cutting the layers remove any detail areas between the leaves or petals, before removing the main background area: this will make the paper easier to handle.

4 Cut individual leaves, fruit or flowers from the border for the third layer, then attach them to the second layer using very small blobs of silicone.

Cutting the flowers

1 Cut the flower cluster, stalk and leaves in one piece: this is the base layer. If the design has a shadow, do not include it as part of the picture. Next, secure the base layer on to the centre of the textured paper, using glue or spray adhesive to do this.

2 Cut the second layer the same as the base layer, including all parts of the design. Apply blobs of silicone on to the base layer, then position the second layer on top, making sure it is positioned exactly over the base layer.

3 Cut out the flower cluster again, omitting several flower heads: each time you omit part of the design it will recede into the background. Fix the third layer in place using silicone.

4 To give the design depth you will need about another four layers. On subsequent layers omit more flower heads. For the last few layers, use single flower heads, building up the height on some more than others (see the step-by-step diagrams on the following page). Before attaching the last layer, shape

Cutting the flowers

1 Cut the complete flower for the base and second layer.

2 For the third layer, cut the flower cluster from the paper, then carefully remove the flower heads that are furthest away.

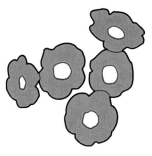

3 For the fourth layer, cut away more heads, taking care that the areas between the flowers are the same on all layers.

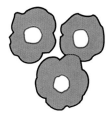

4 For the fifth and subsequent layers, keep reducing the number of heads until you are cutting individual flowers.

the petals to give them life and form, using a shaping tool or spoon. To do this, lay the paper face up on a shaping pad or cutting mat and then, using a shaping tool or spoon handle, gently rub the paper in a circular movement following the shape of the petals to give them a concave appearance (see Finishing Techniques, page 26). Do not press too hard or the paper will crease. Fix the final layer in place using silicone.

Cutting the leaves

1 The base and first layer of the leaves are already in position, so now is the time to decide how you will position the subsequent layers. Cut out the leaves in one piece, then study their positions: some will be further back than others. Cut away the leaves that are furthest away, then fix this second layer in place using silicone.

2 Repeat the process, removing the leaves that are furthest back as you cut each layer. The final layer should be single leaves: shape the edges to give them form in the same way as the flowers. Build up the layers of leaves to the same level as the flower head.

Assembling the picture

1 When the silicone is dry, assemble the picture in the frame. Replace the glass as this will help to protect the picture from dust and dirt.

Making the gift box

1 Following the measurements on page 181, draw a box shape on to thin card. Cut out the shape following the solid lines.

2 Score along the broken lines with the back of a blunt knife and then fold the card backwards along the scored lines, forming the box shape. Open out the box and lay it on a flat surface.

Cutting the flowers

1 Cut out the base layer of the flowers and leaves and stick it centrally on the box front using glue or spray adhesive.

2 Cut out a second layer, exactly the same as the base layer, then carefully attach it to the base using blobs of silicone.

3 Build up the layers, removing petals in the same way as you did for the picture. You will need at least another five layers, omitting more petals on each layer.

4 The stalk, bud and leaves should only have two or three layers as they are behind the main flower heads.

5 On the top layers, curl the individual petals under at the tips using the shaping tool or spoon (see Finishing Techniques, page 26); attach the petals to the box.

Assembling the box

1 To assemble the box: re-fold along the scored lines, then use double-sided sticky tape to attach the tabs to the base and sides.

Making the tag

1 Make a tracing of the template opposite, and cut a gift tag from card, then using a punch, make a hole at the top. Cut out two small flower heads from the gift-wrap, then découpage them on to the tag. Thread the tag with a length of ribbon.

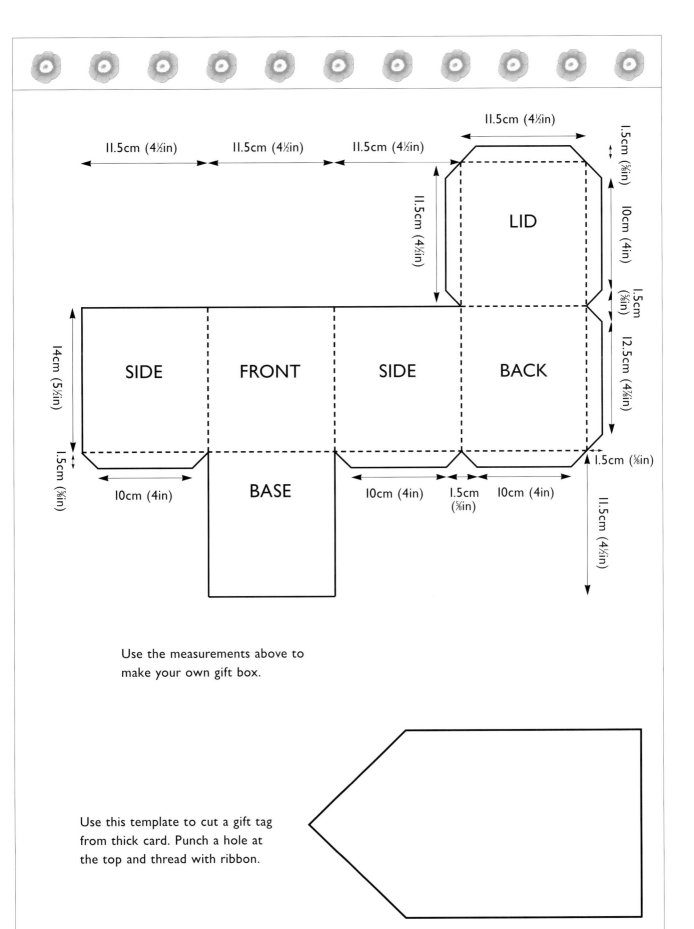

11.5cm (4½in)

11.5cm (4½in)   11.5cm (4½in)   11.5cm (4½in)

1.5cm (⅝in)

11.5cm (4½in)

10cm (4in)

LID

11.5cm (4½in)

1.5cm (⅝in)

12.5cm (4⅞in)

14cm (5½in)

SIDE   FRONT   SIDE   BACK

1.5cm (⅝in)

1.5cm (⅝in)

10cm (4in)

BASE

10cm (4in)   1.5cm (⅝in)   10cm (4in)

11.5cm (4½in)

Use the measurements above to make your own gift box.

Use this template to cut a gift tag from thick card. Punch a hole at the top and thread with ribbon.

Marbled Frame

Creating beautiful marbled paper is very easy using oil paints and wallpaper paste. Each sheet of paper that you make will be unique. Once dry, the paper made here has been used to cover a picture frame and hexagonal box, which have been further decorated with a daisy flower motif. (See Techniques page 10)

You will need

- Flat MDF frame 30x40cm (12x16in)
- Hexagonal-shaped box
- Paper (good quality drawing paper)
- Card – thin, cream-coloured
- Paper for making pulp
- Oil paints or marbling paints –
  rose, flesh, magenta, blue
- Turpentine, wallpaper paste
- Light-coloured raffia, mount board
- Plastic tray to use as a vat and
  marbling tray
- Kitchen cloths, hardboard rectangles, weights
- Beetroot – cooked (not in vinegar)
- Food colourings – yellow and green
- Gold rubbing paste
- Teaspoon or pipette, thin wire (coat hanger)
- Mould and deckle, newspaper
- Bucket, length of wood or hand-held liquidizer
- Tacky glue, masking tape, paintbrushes
- Craft knife, pencil, ruler, scissors, water jar

Preparing the marbling tray

1 Before beginning, protect your work surface with several layers of newspaper because oil paints can mark surfaces and clothing.

2 Mix the wallpaper paste, following the instructions on the packet for making 'size'. Make enough paste to three quarters fill your tray. Leave to stand until the paste reaches room temperature.

3 Cut ten pieces of drawing paper to fit inside the tray, or use handmade paper (see Making a Sheet of Paper, page 13).

4 To marble the paper you can use oil or specialist marbling paints: oil paints are messier to use than marbling paints, but give a brighter, sharper colour. The oils will need to be mixed with a little turpentine to make the paint more liquid.

5 In a saucer, mix magenta with a little flesh colouring, and add a small amount to the wallpaper paste. Then add a tiny spot of blue. Using a teaspoon or a pipette, add equal drops of this mix to the surface of the paste. The colour should spread about 2.5cm (1in) across the paste. If the paint does not spread, then thin it with a little more turpentine; if it spreads too far and too thinly, add more undiluted paint; if the colours sink, the paste

may be too thick, and it will need to be thinned with a little water.

6 Using a thin piece of wire, gently swirl the paint around in the tray until you are satisfied with the design. Do this very carefully so that the paint stays on top of the paste.

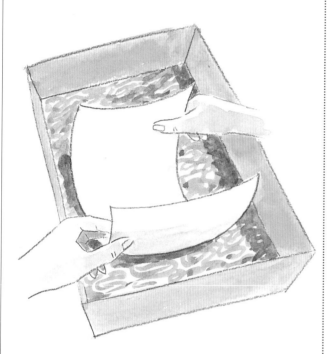

Making the marbled paper

1 Hold one of the pieces of paper that you cut to size by diagonal corners. Lower the paper on to the surface of the vat belly first, and then let the corners gently down in a rolling motion. This will prevent air bubbles getting trapped under the paper, which will leave white marks in the marbled design.

2 The paper will soak up the paint almost immediately. Take the paper out of the vat, holding it by the two corners on the long side, and lay it colour side up on newspaper.

3 Take the marbled paper to a sink or bath and run it under cold running water,

preferably a shower spray. Dry the paper flat on newspaper or hang it on a washing line: it may take two or three days to dry. Flatten the paper under heavy weights before using.

4 Before making the next sheet of paper, skim any remaining paint off the surface of the paste, and then add more paint as before.

5 Make enough paper with a similar pattern to cover the frame and hexagonal box.

Covering the frame

1 Lay the paper on the frame; if the paper is large enough you will be able to cover the frame in four pieces, with a mitre at each corner. If you have to cover each side using several strips of paper, make sure the overlaps are on the diagonal. Glue the paper on to the frame, smoothing out any air bubbles. Once the glue is dry, cover the reverse side of the frame in the same way.

Making paper

1 Make ten sheets of natural-coloured paper (see Making a Sheet of Paper, page 13). Recycle only light-coloured paper with long fibres. Raffia is added to the pulp to give it texture. The raffia should be cut into short lengths and then torn into shreds, before being added to the surface of the pulp for each sheet of paper (see Making Decorative Paper, page 17).

Making the daisy picture

1 Cut a piece of mount board to fit snugly within the hole in the picture frame: this will be the back of the daisy picture. Cut a piece of natural handmade paper the same size as the board, and glue it in place.

2 Tear a rectangle of handmade paper smaller than the backing board, but large enough

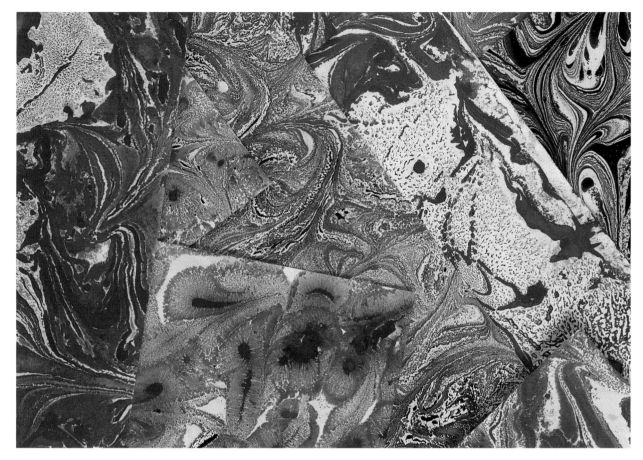

to fit behind the daisy picture (see template on page 187). To make the paper easier to tear, fold the paper where you would like the tear to be, and then dampen it with water before tearing. Do not use scissors or a knife to cut the paper as they will not produce an uneven edge.

3 Extract the juice from the cooked beetroot by cutting it up and allowing the juice to drain down through a strainer.

4 Place the torn rectangle of handmade paper on a piece of scrap paper and then dampen it with water. Using a teaspoon or pipette, apply drops of beetroot juice to the surface of the paper working from the middle. The damp paper will soak up the juice fairly evenly, but you may need to keep adding juice to achieve a strong colour. The strongest colour should be

in the middle of the paper, fading to a paler pink at the edges. Once dry, glue the paper to the centre of the covered backing board.

5 Make tracings of the daisies, leaves and stem on page 187. Cut out the tracings and then lay them on to the natural-coloured paper. Draw around the edges, transferring the designs on to the paper. Cut out the shapes.

6 Dampen the centres of the daisies, leaves and stem with water. Apply a few drops of yellow food colouring to the centre of the daisies, and green and yellow to the leaves and stem.

7 Once the paper is dry, apply gold rubbing paste with an old paintbrush or cotton bud to the edges of the design, and to add detail to the flowers, stem and leaves.

8 Arrange the stem, leaves and daisies on to the beetroot-stained paper, and glue in place.

9 Put the completed picture in to the frame and secure the back with masking tape.

Covering the hexagonal box

1 Make enough marbled paper to cover the hexagonal box and lid. Cut a separate strip for each side of the box, allowing enough to turn over at the top and bottom. Cut a big enough piece of paper to cover the box top and sides, and extra to turn on to the inside. Apply a thin layer of glue to the box and then attach the paper sides, smoothing them down to remove any air bubbles. Glue paper on to the lid, cutting it up to the card at each corner. Turn the excess over, and glue on to the inside of the lid. Cover the bottom, and the inside of the box and lid.

Making the daisy panels

1 Tear eight rectangles of the natural-coloured paper slightly smaller than the sides of the box – remember to fold the paper and dampen it before tearing. Once dry, glue the squares to the centre of each box side.

2 Tear eight more rectangles, slightly smaller than the first. Stain them with beetroot juice in the same way as before, and glue them in the centre of the natural-coloured rectangles.

3 Make a tracing of the small daisy design on the opposite page and use it to cut eight daisies from the natural-coloured paper. Colour the centres with yellow food colouring, and add detail at the edges and centre with gold rubbing paste. Glue a daisy on to the centre of each rectangle.

4 From the natural-coloured paper, tear a hexagon slightly smaller than the box lid, and glue it on to the centre of the lid. Tear another hexagon slightly smaller than the first; dampen it with water and then colour with beetroot juice as before. When dry, glue it to the centre of the natural paper panel. Cut a daisy from natural-coloured paper. Colour the centre and edges as before, and then glue to the centre of the lid.

Making the tags

1 Cut two pieces of thin cream-coloured card 7.5x8.5cm (3x3½in).

2 Tear two pieces of natural-coloured paper, large enough to just overlap the edges of the card; glue one on to each card.

3 For the cream daisy tag, tear a piece of natural-coloured paper 5x6cm (2x2½in). Colour with beetroot juice as before, and then glue to the centre of the tag.

4 Cut a small daisy from natural-coloured paper, colouring the centre with yellow, and then adding detail to the edges with gold. Glue the daisy on to the tag.

5 For the larger daisy tag, make a tracing of the larger single daisy on the opposite page. Cut the daisy from natural-coloured paper, and then colour with beetroot juice.

6 Tear a small circle of natural-coloured paper to fit the centre of the daisy. Colour with yellow food colouring, and then add detail with gold rubbing paste. Glue the circle on to the daisy, and the daisy on to the tag.

7 Punch two holes in the middle of one short side of each tag. Cut two lengths of raffia 25cm (10in) long. Thread raffia twice through the holes in one of the tags, before tying the ends in a knot. Repeat for the other tag.

Large Daisy Tag

Box Top
and
Picture

Small Daisy Tag

Use these outlines to cut daisy shapes from
handmade paper.

Suppliers

UK

Fred Aldous Ltd
37 Lever Street
Manchester
M1 1LW
tel: 08707 517 300
fax: 08707 517 303
email: Aldous@btinternet.com
website: www.fredaldous.co.uk
craft materials
mail order

Art Express
Index House
70 Burley Road
Leeds LS3 1JX
tel: 0800 731 4185
website: www.artexpress.co.uk
art and craft supplies including paper,
paints and display materials

Colart Fine Art & Graphics Ltd
Whitefriars Avenue
Harrow
Middlesex HA3 5RH
tel: 0181 427 4343
paint wholesaler – telephone for local stockist

Crafts World (Head Office Only)
No 8 North Street
Guildford
Surrey GU1 4AF
tel: 07000 757070
retail shops nationwide –
telephone for local store
craft supplies

Hobby Crafts (Head Office Only)
River Court
Southern Sector
Bournemouth International Airport
Christchurch
Dorset BH23 6SE
tel: 0800 272387 freephone
Retail shops nationwide –
telephone for local store
craft supplies

Homecrafts Direct
PO Box 38
Leicester LE1 9BU
tel: 0116 269 77 33
website: www.homecrafts.co.uk
art and craft supplies

Paperchase
213 Tottenham Court Road
83/84 Long Acre
London WC2E
tel: 020 7379 6850
specialists in paper supplies

Stamp Addicts
Park Lane Lodge
Park Lane
Gamlingay
Bedfordshire
SG19 3PD
tel/fax: 01767 650329
email: info@stampaddicts.co.uk
website: www.stampaddicts.com
specialists in rubber stamps, inkpads
and accessories

US

Art2Art
432 Culver Blvd.
Playa Del Rey, CA 90293
tel: (877) 427-2383
fax: (310) 827-8111
website: www.art2art.com
craft supplies

DecoArt
P.O. Box 386
Stanford, KY 40484-0360
tel: 1-606-365-3193
fax: 1-606-365-9739
email: paint@decoart.com
website: www.decoart.com
acrylic paints

Judi-Kins
17803 South Harvard Blvd
Gardena, CA 90248
tel: (310) 515-1115
fax: (310) 323-6619
website: www.judikins.com
stamps and stamping supplies

Kate's Paperie
1282 Third Ave
New York, NY 10021
tel: (212) 396-3670
fax: (212) 941-9560
email: info@katespaperie.com
website: www.katespaperie.com
decorative papers and stationery supplies

The Paper Source
232 W. Chicago Avenue
Chicago, IL 60610
tel: (312) 337-0798
fax: (312) 337-0741
stationery supplies

Plaid Enterprises, Inc
3225 Westech Drive
Norcross, GA 30092-3500
tel: (800) 842-4197
website: www.plaidonline.com
craft supplies

Rugg Road Paper
105 Charles Street
Boston, MA 02114
tel: (617) 742-0002
decorative papers and stationery supplies

ACKNOWLEDGMENTS

Thanks to the following designers for contributing their projects to this title:

Michael Ball
St Basil's Pen Tidy (p136)

Janet Bridge
Citrus Bags and Paper (p98)

Jan Cox and John Underwood
3-D Greetings (p70), Moon and Star Cards (p84), Pansy Gift Tags (p110), Fold 'n' Dye Gift Bags (p114), Batik-Covered Books (p132), Scrap Paper Photo Albums (p152)

Jill Millis
Glittering Christmas Cards (p74), Organic Nature Cards (p78), Notes from the Garden (p88), Black Cat Accessories (p126), Geometric Trinket Boxes (p172)

Jill Millis and Jan Cox
Marbled Frame (p182)

Cheryl Owen
Bright Daisy Cards (p62), Lacy Wrapping and Cards (p94), Vegetable Caskets (p106), Spiral Stamps (p158), Native American Trays (p160), Botanical Picture and Box (p176)

Rachel Owens
Miniature Scrap Ideas (p66)

Susan Penny
Strawberry Gift Holders (p102), Petal and Leaf Writing Set (p180)

Lynne Strange
Mini Gift Bowls (p120), Circus Fun Desk Set (p142)

Lynne Strange and Susan Penny
Embellished Rose Casket (p164)

Index